Colorado

HERITAGE OF THE HIGHEST STATE

Colorado

HERITAGE OF THE
HIGHEST STATE

Fay D. Metcalf • Thomas J. Noel • Duane A. Smith

PRUETT **P** PUBLISHING COMPANY
Boulder, Colorado

First Edition
    4 5 6 7 8 9

Printed in the United States of America

Library of Congress Cataloging in Publication Data

Metcalf, Fay D., 1928–
  Colorado: heritage of the highest state.

  Bibliography: p.
  Includes index.
  Summary: A history of Colorado from earliest times
to the present.
    1. Colorado—History—Juvenile literature.
[1. Colorado—History] I. Noel, Thomas J. (Thomas
Jacob) II. Smith, Duane A. III. Title.
F776.3.M47 1984   978.8   83-17707
ISBN 0-87108-255-1

Acknowledgments

The authors of *Colorado: Heritage of the Highest State* greatly appreciate help from teachers all over the state. They reviewed this book, making corrections and suggestions. We welcome ongoing advice from teachers, students, and others interested in making this a better and more useful book.

Chuck Woodward and Carl Cordova of Gateway High School, Nancy Gregory and Ray Jenkins of Hinkley High School, Jerry Fabyanic and Pat Heist Ward of Aurora Hills Middle School, and Nancy Allen of the Education Department of the Colorado Heritage Center have been especially helpful.

Pam Burns of Sacred Heart Junior High School in Boulder and Lynn Brown, Ward Lee, and Brent Brown of Smiley and Miller Junior High Schools in Durango and Colorado history students Mike Ferguson, Virginia Shannon, and Laralee Smith also helped make this a better book.

Finally, Gerald Keenan and Merilee Eggleston suggested, edited, and helped bring this book into your hands.

Contents

Introduction

Colorado's history is short—the written record goes back only about 200 years—but exciting. It includes booms and busts in farming and ranching, gold and silver, water and oil. And it is filled with characters, such as Father Escalante, the Spanish priest who first explored and mapped much of Colorado, and Ouray, the Ute chief who fought for peace. Clara Brown, a former black slave, made enough money washing miners' jeans to help her people build churches and become successful pioneers. Elizabeth Iliff came to Colorado selling Singer sewing machines and wound up running the state's most famous ranch. Josephine Roche, a pioneer policewoman, became a mine owner and ran for governor. Horace Tabor took millions out of his mines only to sink his fortune back in the ground and lose it all.

In each chapter of this book, you will find some questions, activities, and reading suggestions to help you learn more of Colorado's story than we can present here.

Enjoy your reading. You will discover a high, dry, and handsome state whose rugged natural beauty and colorful history are well worth knowing and conserving.

Unit I

Colorado		United States	
	25000 B.C.		Asiatic People cross Bering Strait to settle in North America
1300	Anasazi abandon Mesa Verde	1300	Norseman may have reached North America
1776	Dominguez-Escalante Expedition	1776	Declaration of Independence
1806	Zebulon Pike Expedition	1803	Louisiana Purchase
1820	Stephen Long Expedition	1812	War of 1812
1832	Bent's Old Fort built	1820s	Santa Fe Trail Trade

—1—
The Land

Colorado is an amazing land. It is the only state that is an almost perfect rectangle. At its widest Colorado is 387 miles east to west and 276 miles north to south. It ranks as the eighth largest state in the United States and has a total area of 104,247 square miles.

Colorado became a state in 1876, the same year the United States celebrated its centennial, or 100th birthday. That is how Colorado got its nickname, the Centennial State. The state is divided into sixty-three counties, with Las Animas and Moffat the largest and Denver and Gilpin the smallest. In each county one town is designated the county seat. Denver is the state capital and Colorado's largest city.

Colorado is the highest state in the union. The average elevation is 6,800 feet above sea level. But, if we leveled out Colorado to an average elevation of 1,000 feet, what do you think would happen? Colorado might be the biggest state in the United States—bigger than Texas or Alaska.

Mount Elbert (14,431 ft.) is the highest point in Colorado and the fourteenth tallest mountain in the nation. Alaska has twelve taller mountains and California has one. Colorado, however, has fifty-four peaks that are 14,000 feet or higher. The lowest point in the state is in the Arkansas Valley near Holly; it is 3,350 feet.

It snows somewhere in Colorado every month of the year. Leadville has had several snowfalls on July 4. You may have been picnicking in the mountains some summer day when snow fell. Colorado holds the world's record for the most snowfall in twenty-four hours: seventy-six inches at Silver Lake in April 1921.

Colorado is called the "mother of rivers" because so many waterways start in our mountains. Rivers radiate out of the state like the spokes of a wheel. The mighty Colorado River starts here and flows 1,450 miles to reach the ocean. The Rio Grande (Grand River in Spanish) is even longer, 1,885 miles. Rivers from Colorado flow into both the Pacific Ocean and the Gulf of Mexico. Near Poncha Pass, something very unusual occurs. From starting points that are within a few feet of each other, water flows in three different directions toward the sea. Part of it flows into the Colorado River, some into the Rio Grande, and the rest eventually ends up in the Mississippi River. Water a stone's throw apart at the start will be separated by thousands of miles when it finally reaches its destination. Rivers, as we shall see, have played a very important role in Colorado's history. Settlers, animals, and industry all need water.

Because Colorado is so varied in its climate and elevation, it has recorded some very unusual temperatures. The coldest was a frigid sixty degrees below zero at the Taylor Park Dam in Gunnison County. The hottest was a torrid 118 degrees at Bennett. Did you know that the difference in the average July temperature between the towns of Lamar (eastern plains) and Fraser (mountains) in Colorado is almost the same as that between Denver and Nome, Alaska? From the eastern plains to the high mountain peaks, to the plateaus and river valleys of western Colorado, this is a beautiful and fascinating state.

It is no wonder, then, that a young college professor, Katherine Lee Bates, was moved to write these lines in her poem "America the Beautiful." She stood on top of Pike's Peak in 1893. "I was looking out over the sea-like expanse of fertile country," she said, when the opening lines "floated into my mind."

O beautiful for spacious skies,
For amber waves of grain,
For purple mountain majesties
Above the fruited plain!

She was impressed. So were millions of others when they saw the wonders of Colorado. If you have not traveled around the state, try to do so. Few other states can offer such breathtaking scenery, varied animal and plant life, and a variety of climates.

Colorado's geography has played a very important role in the history and development of the state. Farming, mining, ranching, tourism, townbuilding, industry, and transportation have all been shaped by geography.

Eastern Plains

Look at Colorado's geographic regions. The state divides itself naturally into three parts. The first region to be seen by most early visitors was the eastern plains. These are a natural extension of the region called the Great Plains, which start back in Kansas and Nebraska.

The plains slope gently upward from Colorado's eastern border to an elevation of 6,000 feet. They come as far as an imaginary line running from Fort Collins to Boulder, Denver, and Pueblo. Rainfall is scant in this region. It is also windy in the spring and has been known for its dust storms, heat, and summer droughts. Because of these and the sparse summer vegetation, early visitors were fooled into calling the plains the "Great American Desert." They are not. It just seemed that way to people who were used to the well-watered, lush green of the eastern United States.

The eastern plains of Colorado were home to the buffalo before the cattlemen arrived. Water is the key to development here and throughout the state. —Richard L. Gilbert

Colorado's Rivers

South Platte River

South Fork Republican River

Arkansas River

Purgatoire River

North Platte River

Rio Grande

Yampa River

White River

Colorado River

Gunnison River

Animas River

Dolores River

SEDGWICK
PHILLIPS
YUMA
LOGAN
WASHINGTON
MORGAN
WELD
LARIMER
JACKSON
ROUTT
MOFFAT
RIO BLANCO
GARFIELD
MESA
GRAND
EAGLE
PITKIN
SUMMIT
BOULDER
GILPIN
CLEAR-CREEK
JEFFER-SON
ADAMS
DENVER
ARAPAHOE
ELBERT
DOUGLAS
PARK
LAKE
CHAFFEE
DELTA
GUNNISON
MONTROSE
OURAY
SAN MIGUEL
DOLORES
MONTEZUMA
LA PLATA
SAN JUAN
HINSDALE
MINERAL
SAGUACHE
RIO GRANDE
ARCHULETA
CONEJOS
ALAMOSA
COSTILLA
HUERFANO
CUSTER
FREMONT
TELLER
EL PASO
DOUGLAS
LINCOLN
KIT CARSON
CHEYENNE
KIOWA
CROWLEY
PUEBLO
OTERO
BENT
PROWERS
LAS ANIMAS
BACA

© American Map Co., Inc. – 18822

Parks, Mountains, Mountain Ranges and Mesas

Continental Divide

SEDGWICK
PHILLIPS
YUMA
LOGAN
WASHINGTON
MORGAN
WELD
KIT CARSON
CHEYENNE
KIOWA
LINCOLN
ADAMS
ARAPAHOE
DENVER
ELBERT
DOUGLAS
EL PASO
TELLER
Pike's Peak
PROWERS
BENT
OTERO
CROWLEY
PUEBLO
LAS ANIMAS
BACA
Front Range
Medicine Bow
Middle Park
Rabbit Ears
North Park
Gore
North Park
GILPIN
CLEAR-CREEK
SUMMIT
PARK
South Park
Mosquito
Sawatch
FREMONT
CUSTER
Wet
Sangre de Cristo
HUERFANO
COSTILLA
ALAMOSA
San Luis Valley
RIO GRANDE
CONEJOS
ARCHULETA
Continental Divide
LARIMER
JACKSON
ROUTT
GRAND
JEFFER-SON
CHAFFEE
SAGUACHE
MINERAL
Elk
Grand Mesa
EAGLE
PITKIN
GUNNISON
HINSDALE
OURAY
SAN JUAN
San Juans
La Platas
Mesa Verde
GARFIELD
RIO BLANCO
MESA
DELTA
MONTROSE
SAN MIGUEL
DOLORES
MONTEZUMA
LA PLATA
MOFFAT

Nutritious native grasses grow abundantly on this prairie land. Buffalo, antelope, and other animals have thrived on it, and numerous Indian peoples roamed over the area to hunt these animals. Because of the rich grass lands, it later became an important ranching center. When the farmers came, they first settled along the rivers, then moved onto the drier land. The eastern plains, because they are lower, have a longer growing season (the number of days between the last frost of spring and the first frost of fall). The region is also well known for its abundant sunshine and is beautiful in its own way.

Mountains

Early visitors and miners were not interested in the plains. They wanted to reach the mountains. Colorado has always been famous for its mountains, especially Pike's Peak, which was our state's first mountain to be named on maps. Tourists have been climbing it or riding to the top for many years. Colorado has more than 1,000 peaks above 10,000 feet. The fifty-four that top 14,000 feet are 79% of all the "fourteeners" in the United States, outside of Alaska. You can see why Colorado is called "the crest of the continent."

How much different is this view of the mountains from the one Stephen Long saw in June 1820. Longmont is in the foreground and Long's Peak in the background, right.
—Richard L. Gilbert

The mountains stretch from the rolling foothills west of Fort Collins, Boulder, Denver, and Colorado Springs to the high Continental Divide, the "backbone" of the Rocky Mountains, and then westward. Continental Divide means a ridge of mountains that divide the water flow between east and west. On the eastern slope, water runs east to the Gulf of Mexico and the Mississippi River. On the western slope it eventually reaches the Pacific Ocean.

The Rocky Mountains, which cut across central Colorado from north to south, are part of a larger chain of mountains. These mountains run from Canada into Mexico. In Colorado, the Rocky Mountains reach their highest elevation and greatest width. Within the Rockies or near them are other smaller ranges. Colorado has the Sangre de Cristo Range (Blood of Christ, named by the Spanish), the La Platas (silver), the San Juans, the Medicine Bow Range, the Sawatch Mountains, and others. One of the best-named ranges is the Never Summer in Rocky Mountain National Park.

The rivers have cut some impressive canyons while trying to break out of these vast mountains. Of these, the Royal Gorge of the Arkansas River is the most famous. It narrows to thirty feet, with cliffs rising 1,200 feet above the river.

Beavers first drew Anglo and French Americans into the mountains. Fur trappers worked all through this region in search of this furry rodent. Grizzly, black, and brown bears, deer, mountain sheep, and mountain lions were once plentiful also. Many of them were hunted nearly to extinction before people realized what was happening. These animals were important to the Indians. To later Americans of the 1900s the buffalo, deer, and beaver were most important; their skins could be sold to make hats, blankets, and clothes. Buffalo and deer were also a source of meat, and beaver tail was a special treat.

Western Slope

The part of Colorado west of the Continental Divide is known as the Western Slope. It also has mountains— for instance, the very rugged San Juans surrounding Ouray, Silverton, and Telluride, and the Elk Mountains near Crested Butte and Aspen. But this part of the state has some large river valleys as well. Since they were protected from the worst winter storms

and cold, they became centers of farming and ranching. The Gunnison Valley, and the Grand Valley near Grand Junction, are two of the best known. Because it was all by itself west of the mountains, the Western Slope was the last of these three regions to be settled.

The climate, rainfall, and growing seasons of the Western Slope vary greatly. The far western and northwestern parts are semi-arid or almost a desert. They are a hard land for animals and people to live in. Rainfall is very light. On the other hand, it is much wetter in the mountains. Some mountains receive up to 300 inches of snowfall each winter.

The Western Slope is a scenic land. It has high mountains and deserts. It has vast river valleys and huge mesas. Mesa means table in Spanish. Early Spanish explorers gave that name to these land forms. The largest one is Grand Mesa, which rises to 10,000 feet and towers over Grand Junction. Mesa Verde (green tableland), in southwest Colorado is the famous site of cliff dwellings and thousand-year-old Indian villages.

There are also awesome river canyons in western Colorado. The Black Canyon of the Gunnison, not far from Montrose, is a national monument. At its deepest point, the canyon walls tower 2,425 feet. The northwestern part of the Western Slope is wild, lonely country. It was so isolated that it was the very last area of the state to be settled. The far southwestern corner of Colorado is the only place in the United States where four states—New Mexico, Utah, Arizona, and Colorado—come together at one point. Imagine being able to see and touch four states at one time!

DID YOU KNOW?

That Colorado is:

- half the size of France
- 12 times as large as Massachusetts
- about the same size as New York, Ohio, Connecticut and New Hampshire combined
- twice as large as England

Mountain Parks

In the Rocky Mountains of Colorado are found four great "parks." These are flat or gently rolling valleys. They are North Park, Middle Park, South Park, and the San Luis Valley (originally San Luis Park). The San Luis Valley and South Park are the largest.

At one time buffalo and other animals roamed these parks. They were the favorite hunting grounds for Indians and fur trappers. Settlement came to them very early, especially ranching. In the mountains around these valleys minerals were later found. So they were also involved in the mining rushes.

Geography and Settlement

Two geographic features dominate the history of Colorado: the Rocky Mountains and the rivers. In the mountains were found beaver, gold, and silver. These brought people to the future state of Colorado. If enough beavers could be trapped, or enough gold or silver mined, a person could make enough money to retire after just a few years' work.

Because of mining, permanent settlement came. Wagon roads and railroads were built. Farmers and ranchers entered the mountains to furnish food for the miners. Mining camps were started. For forty years after the famous 1859 Pike's Peak gold rush, mining was the most important industry in Colorado.

The rivers were equally important. Without water, people could not stay. This is true of all three regions of Colorado. The ranchers and farmers settled in the river valleys of the mountains and plains. It is no accident that Colorado's largest cities are found along the eastern foothills, where the rivers break out of the mountains. Here also are concentrated Colorado's commerce and industry. These well-watered river valleys were the best places in which to settle. The canyons also served as gateways into the mountains. This is true on the Western Slope as well. Grand Junction, Durango, Gunnison, and Montrose, for example, were established along rivers.

Settlement then followed several basic geographic patterns:

1. Towns on the canyon routes into the mountains. (Denver)

2. Settlements along the rivers across the eastern plains. (Greeley)

3. Camps and towns near the mineral outcroppings of gold, silver, and coal. (Central City)

4. Towns on agricultural sites and transportation routes. (Las Animas)

5. Health or tourist resorts near scenic or unique geographic features. (Glenwood Springs, health; Estes Park, tourist)

Think about the settlements in your county. Did they follow one or more of these patterns?

Water

Colorado averages 16.6 inches of rainfall (including snow) yearly. As we mentioned, however, this amount can change greatly from year to year. Fortunately, the mountain snowpack and runoff can be used for irrigation during the spring and summer. All the water the state has comes from rainfall, snowfall, and out of the rivers that have their headwaters in Colorado. Neighboring states can get their water from rivers flowing into and through them; Colorado cannot. Hardly any water enters Colorado from other states. In this respect it is unique.

Water is Colorado's most valuable natural resource. And although many great rivers start in the state's mountains, we do not have the right to use all that water. Colorado must share its water with neighboring states.

Seasons

People like to live in Colorado, as its growth over the years shows. Generally, Colorado's temperatures are mild—it is rarely too hot or too cold for very long. It is usually very dry—there is hardly ever enough moisture in the air (humidity) to make you feel uncomfortable. Colorado is famous for its climate, and the lack of humidity is the main reason it is so pleasant.

Colorado's changing seasons give variety to its climate. There are only three, really—fall, winter, and summer. James Grafton Rogers, in his book, *My Rocky Mountain Valley,* explains why:

> The four seasons, spring, summer, autumn and winter, are terms that belong to the language of Europe and of Eastern North America . . . . There is, in the Rocky Mountains, no gentle spring, no gradual awakening of life, no slow emergence of vegetation. Summer comes suddenly, some day in early June, on the heels of winter.

Summer is the season in which the plants flourish and the animals are intensely active. They have to gather much of their food for the rest of the year. Fall lasts until about Christmas. The aspen turn yellow and the snows start to come.

Winter snows bury spring. As Rogers wrote, "Our winter is not gloomy or snowbound. It takes turns with sunshine and snow storms." Then summer arrives and, in a way, starts the new year, not the calendar date of January 1.

These seasons are important to Colorado. In "spring" and summer the crops must be planted and nurtured. The growing season ranges from 76 to nearly 200 days. Farmers have to be careful what they plant to be sure that it has time to grow to maturity. Fall is a good season to tour Colorado. It is the time when the crops are harvested (and winter wheat is planted) and the wild animals are preparing for the oncoming winter, which can be severe. The first Coloradans were often isolated from each other by severe storms and heavy snows. Towns were cut off on occasion also.

Winter can still do that. In 1982, a Christmas eve blizzard paralyzed Denver when two feet of snow fell, but this was not the biggest of all Denver blizzards. That one came in December 1913, when the city received 47.7 inches of snow with drifts up to twenty feet high. Digging out was a tough job. Hundreds of men were paid $2.50 per day to shovel snow and load it into horse-drawn wagons. Some of the snow piles they made did not melt until summer.

Today people do not feel so alone as they did in those earlier blizzards. Telephones, radios, and television keep them in touch with each other. In fact, winter has actually helped the state. It has become one of the biggest tourist seasons, now that Colorado skiing is world famous.

State Emblems

Like other states, Colorado has its official state flower, bird, nickname, and so forth. You will find these listed in this chapter in a special section. In a state as large and varied as this one, it was hard to select these emblems. James Grafton Rogers tells why:

> The Blue columbine is called the Colorado State flower but a single symbol is hard to find for a region so varied as ours, so full of wet and dry, high and low, hot and cold extremes. The columbine grows only in the mountains, less than half the state . . . .
>
> While the State flower and the State tree [Colorado Blue Spruce] are mountain dwellers, the bird, chosen by a vote of school children as a symbol for the commonwealth, lives on the plains and is scarcely known to mountain people. It is the lark bunting, a little black and white bird with a brilliant song.

Students of your age and younger helped to select the lark bunting, and in 1891 they also chose the columbine.

In 1981 and 1982 two groups of fourth graders worked hard to have a state fossil named. They were from the McElwain Elementary School in Thornton. In 1982 they persuaded Governor Richard Lamm to choose the stegosaurus ("Steggy"), although the state legislature balked at the idea. "Steggy," all several tons of him, is the heavyweight of all the state emblems.

Millions of years ago, the stegosaurus and other dinosaurs roamed over what would become Colorado. The climate, land forms, vegetation, and rivers—everything—were different back then. No one living today ever saw dinosaurs, but we know they existed and much about them. Dinosaur bones have been found throughout the state, and the first complete stegosaurus skeleton was discovered in Colorado. That is a major reason it was selected to be the state fossil.

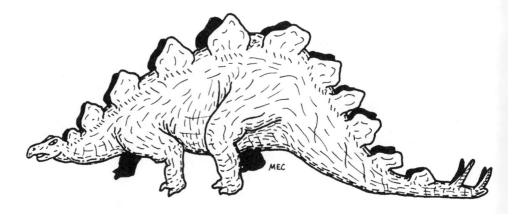

Colorado

Colorado is a wondrous, fascinating land, a land to be explored. Its geography has played a major role in its history. This has been true from the days of the Mesa Verde Indians until today.

In the words of the chorus of the state song, "Where the Columbines Grow":

'Tis the land where the columbines grow,
Overlooking the plains far below,
While the cool summer breeze in the evergreen trees
Softly sings where the columbines grow.

Colorado has to be seen, felt, studied, and explored to be understood. The following chapters will give you a start.

STATE EMBLEMS

Colorado	—state named for Colorado River; Colorado is Spanish for red or ruddy.
Nickname	—Centennial State
Motto	—*Nil Sine Numine:* Nothing without Providence
Flower	—Blue/lavender columbine
Bird	—Lark Bunting
Animal	—Bighorn sheep
Tree	—Colorado blue spruce
Fossil	—Stegosaurus
Song	—"Where the Columbines Grow"
Flag	—Three equal stripes, two blue and a white. A red letter "c" encircling a golden disk is at the left.

QUESTIONS:

1. If someone from another country asked you to describe Colorado, how would you respond? What would you say if a person from another part of Colorado asked you what your section of the state looked like?

2. What is the difference in elevation between the highest and the lowest points in the state?

3. Explain why "mother of rivers" is a good nickname for Colorado.

4. What native animals were found in the various regions of the state?

5. Why were both the mountains and the rivers important to Colorado's development? Explain.

6. What pattern of development did your county follow?

7. What are the most important features of Colorado's climate?

8. How many of Colorado's emblems did you know before you read this chapter?

ACTIVITIES:

1. See if your school library or historical society has old atlases of the state. Check to see if the boundaries of your county have changed over the past hundred years. If they have, make a series of maps that will show the changes and display your maps in the classroom.

2. Make a flour-paste map of your county. Show the topography and make appropriate symbols to show the ways most of the people there make their living.

3. Try to arrange a Saturday trip to the most isolated area you can find near your town. Take along a bird identification book, some binoculars, and a sketch book. Record the number of bird and animal species you find. Report the results to the rest of the class.

4. If mineral ores played an important role in the economic history of your region, read up on the minerals and try to find samples of them to show the class.

5. Find out the source of the water used in your town's system. Then make a map or chart showing how the water moves from its source to the water faucets in the school.

6. Write a poem or song that reflects the Colorado you know best.

Books you might enjoy:

Walter R. Borneman & Lyndon J. Lampert. *A Climbing Guide to Colorado's Fourteeners*. Boulder: Pruett, 1978. Learn all about Colorado's 14,000 ft. mountains.

David Lavender. *David Lavender's Colorado*. New York: Doubleday, 1976. Wonderful photographs and fascinating insights into all parts of the state.

Robert Ormes. *Guide to the Colorado Mountains*. Colorado Springs: World Press, 1979. All you ever wanted to know about mountains.

James Grafton Rogers. *My Rocky Mountain Valley*. Boulder: Pruett, 1968. One of the best books ever written about Colorado's environment.

Joy Clapp & Paul C. Stevens. *Geography of Colorado*. Boulder: The Old West Text Books, 1954 (rev. 1977). A helpful text and workbook with many fill in the blank questions and tear-out maps.

Generalized Archeological Stages
(Southwestern Colorado Only)

Present

HISTORIC

			Some hunting and collecting
			Some horticulture
A.D. 1000 LATE PREHISTORIC	Anasazi	Pueblo Phases	Ceramics statewide
		Basketmaker	Bow and Arrow Continued use of atlatl

1 A.D./B.C.		Atlatl used in hunting
1000 B.C. 2000 B.C.	ARCHAIC	Mixed base subsistence relying on hunting and collecting
3000 B.C. 4000 B.C. 5000 B.C.		

6000 B.C. 7000 B.C.		Spear and atlatl used
8000 B.C. 9000 B.C. 10000 B.C. 11000 B.C.	PALEO-INDIAN	Big game food hunters and food collectors

—2—

The First People of Colorado

The earliest people to live in the land we now call Colorado were hunting and food gathering groups known as Paleo-Indians. *Paleolithic* is a term that is a combination of Greek words meaning ancient stone. So, the Paleo-Indians were ancient people who made stone tools. If it seems strange to you to call a group of people by the name of the tools they made, stop to reflect that you live in what is called the "Nuclear Age."

The best-known of the Paleo-Indians of Colorado were the Clovis and Folsom peoples who lived by hunting large animals such as mammoths and ancient bison, and smaller prehistoric animals such as the camel. These early Indians also gathered native food plants. Later Paleo-Indian groups lived in much the same way, but they hunted smaller forms of bison and such modern animals as elk and deer.

Following the Paleo-Indian period, evidence of humans in Colorado is scant for several thousand years. This time-gap corresponds to a dry climate period that probably drove most of the wandering groups of people to more humid lands where there were more game animals and food plants. But a few people may have stayed in the area. Their descendants may be the groups we call Archaic people (Archaic simply means ancient). They too lived in small, mobile groups and they were

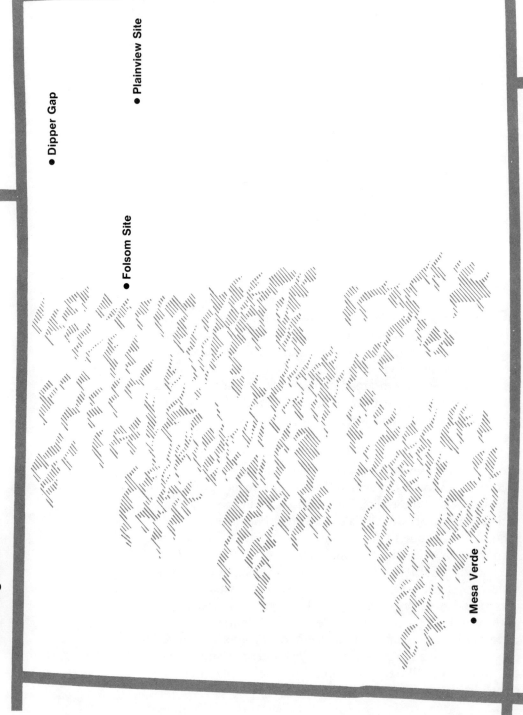

COLORADO
Archeological Sites

● Dipper Gap

● Plainview Site

● Folsom Site

● Mesa Verde

probably more dependent on plants for food than any of the earlier groups. Some of these people were primitive farmers or horticulturists like those who lived in the Mesa Verde area.

All of these groups of people are called prehistoric. This means that they lived before the time of printed records, so our knowledge of them comes from archeologists rather than from historians. Some of this knowledge is guess work. See if you agree with the conclusions drawn.

A Great Find

Geology professor Roy Coffin and his brother Claude spent much of their time doing amateur archeology. One day in 1924, they came across a spear point that was so much larger than any they had seen before that they were convinced they had made a great discovery. They called in experts who told the Coffins they had found a large Folsom site. Most of the spear points and other objects they found had been buried under the seventeen feet of dirt that had blown in over the 10,000 years that separate Folsom people from modern people. When they had completed the excavation, or "dig," the men were able to tell us a little bit about Folsom people.

They used fire. There are many remains of animal bones that had been cooked and then split. All kinds of scraping tools have been found. Perhaps the people used the hides of the animals for clothing and for bags in which to carry their possessions. There were also flaked knives, drills, sandstone rubbing stones, and a few odd tools made of bone. There were no tools of the type used by food collectors or farmers. These people may have depended mainly on meat for their food.

What did Folsom people look like? No one knows. No one has yet found any of the fossil remains of the people. What happened to the people? No one knows that either. The animals they hunted have become extinct. Perhaps as the dry climate period began, and the food source dwindled, the people left the region to find other, better places to live. Perhaps they simply moved to other parts of Colorado.

A Paleo-Indian Bison Hunt

Joe Ben Wheat, an archeologist from the University of Colorado, had studied another group of early Coloradans known as the Plainview people. They occupied many sites in Colorado,

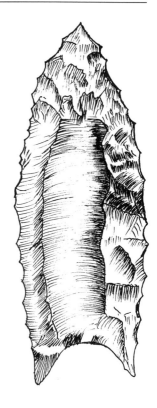

A Folsom Point of the type found by the Coffins.

and they lived some ten thousand or so years ago. In some of their sites, spear points have been found in association with extinct four-pronged antelope; extinct and modern forms of deer and bison; extinct forms of horse, camel, and musk-ox; and with modern forms of woodchuck and mountain sheep. Bones of birds such as the California condor, sand hill cranes, and prairie falcon have also been found. These people may have also been primarily meat eaters. Joe Ben Wheat describes how one large bison kill might have taken place:

> Down in the valley the little stream flowed gently southward. Pleasant groves of trees were heavy with their new burden of early summer leaves. Here and there small herds of bison were drinking. In the lush prairie bottoms paralleling the stream and occasionally crossing it, were the main bison trails.
> To the north, a small herd of 200 to 300 long-horned bison—cows, bulls, yearlings, and young calves—were grazing in the small valley. A gentle breeze was blowing from the south.
> As the bison grazed, a party of hunters approached from the north. Quietly, under cover of the low divide to the west

An early sketch of Bison as they might have appeared to Plainview Peoples.
—Colorado Historical Society

and the steep slope to the east, the hunters began to surround the grazing herd. Moving slowly and cautiously, keeping the breeze in their faces so as not to disturb the keen-nosed animals, they closed in on the herd from the east, north, and west. Escape to the south was blocked by the arroyo. Now the trap was set.

Suddenly the pastoral scene was shattered. At a signal, the hunters rose from their concealment, shouting and yelling, and waving robes to frighten the herd. Spears began to fall among the animals, and at once the bison began a wild stampede toward the south. Too late, the old cows leading the herd saw the arroyo and tried to turn back, but it was impossible. Animal after animal pressed from behind, spurred on by the shower of spears and the shouts of the Indians now in full pursuit. The bison, impeded by the calves, tried to jump the gully, but many fell short and landed in the bottom of it. Others fell kicking, twisting, and turning on top of them, pressing those below ever tighter into the confines of the arroyo. In a matter of seconds, the arroyo was filled to overflowing with a writhing, bellowing mass of bison, forming a living bridge over which a few animals escaped. Now the hunters moved in and began to give the coup de grace to those animals on top, while underneath, the first trapped animals kept up the bellows and groans and their struggle to free themselves, until finally the heavy burden of slain bison above crushed out their lives. In minutes the kill was over.

Over 190 bison were killed that day. The hunters took the best meat from the animals, ate some of it raw, dried some of it for later use, and left the bones and much rotting flesh behind. They also left behind many of the beautifully fashioned Plainview spear points that have given these people their name.

A Plainview Point of the type found near Yuma, Colorado.

The Archaic Indians of Dipper Gap

Later peoples of the plains continued to hunt, but they also seem to have used more intensively other resources from the local environment. The Archaic Indians of Dipper Gap lived about 1500 to 1200 B.C. Were they descendants of the earlier big game hunters? Were they the ancestors of some of the later Plains Indians? No one knows for sure. See what you think. See if you can reconstruct life in Dipper Gap as it was lived such a long time ago. Here is some information from the archeologist's technical report.

The Site as it appeared before excavation.

Surveying the Site.

Digging begins.

The Archeologist explains procedures.

The Dipper Gap living area begins to appear.

A marker used to record steps in the excavation.

1. The Dipper Gap site is named for a local topographical feature. North of the site is a valley called the "dipper" because it has so many springs. A long butte forms the southern boundary of this valley and a large breach in this butte is known as Dipper Gap.

2. Three major springs are located within three miles of the site. Several small seeps located on the butte provide slow, but continuous trickles of water as well. The flat surfaces of the buttes in the area are weathered extensively, forming numerous potholes or depressions in the rock. Filling quickly in the often violent summer thunderstorms, these depressions hold water for several weeks. Several of these potholes are adjacent to the Dipper Gap site.

3. Summers are hot and there are only a few lasting cold spells in winter. Climate on the plains since the dry spell is assumed to have been one of periodic change between conditions somewhat moister than present, and drier periods such as the drought of the 1930s.

4. No Paleo-Indian sites are reported in the area, but surface specimens of projectile points (spear points) from all known Paleo-Indian sites are contained in the collections of local "arrowhead" collectors.

5. The prehistoric record from excavated sites suggests the Dipper Gap site was occupied about 1500 B.C. Other nearby sites contain points dating 1000 B.C. to A.D. 1300. After this there is no evidence of human occupation until historic times.

Projectile Points found at Dipper Gap.

6. Artifacts found at this site include:

21 Hearths—Several were built above others, indicating many occupations of the site.

Mineral Paint—numerous small pieces and one large piece each of hematite and limonite.

Chipped Stone Artifacts:
    106 identifiable points
    171 identifiable biface tools
    90 end scrapers
    82 side scrapers
    53 drills, perforators, and gravers
    42 core choppers
    66 plant milling tools
    1 shaft smoother

Bone Artifacts:
    2 metapoidal awls
    1 scapula awl
    3 scapula scraping tools
    1 bird bone bead
    6 incised bone discs (gaming pieces)

Animal Bones (all show signs of butchering):
    bison—10 animals?   rabbit—several
    ground squirrel—several   marmot—several
    dog or coyote—2 or more   antelope—2 +
    deer—several   turtle—1
    English sparrow—1   rodent—1

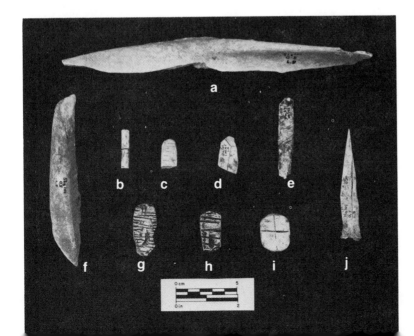

Tools found at Dipper Gap:
a. Bison Scapula Awl
b. Bird Bone Bead
c. Gaming Piece
d. Turtle Shell
e. Bone with marks from butchering
f. Bone Scraper
g., h., i. Gaming pieces
j. Bowe Awl

What makes the lives of these people different from the Paleo-Indians? If you would like to check your guesses with the archeological interpretation, turn to appendix A and read the archeologist's summary.

Mesa Verde: The Green Tableland

All over the southwest the *mesa* or flat-topped mountain may be found. Sharp cliffs of red, tan, and brown sandstone are surrounded by more gentle slopes of light-colored earth. These rock cliffs were first laid down as sand dunes and as shallow sea deposits. Then, through the ages they became compacted into thick layers of sandstone and shale. During century after century and in many stages, the earth's crust was thrust upward, making towering plateaus.

Then, immediately, erosion began. The dry, thin atmosphere of these high altitudes permitted temperature extremes which began to weaken the compacted sandstone. Torrential rains, "gully washers" we call them in Colorado, carried away gravel, sand, and even large boulders down the arroyos. As this happened time after time through thousands of years, ravines and canyons formed. Sometimes the force undercut the sharp cliffs and eventually huge caves were formed as the sides of some of the canyons.

The land was high, about 8,500 feet, and there were heavy seasonal rains. This meant that pinon and juniper and shrubs and seed plants could develop and survive on these mesas. With this vegetation providing a dependable food supply, wild game came into the area. When the ancestors of the cliff dwellers entered the region some 2,000 to 10,000 years ago, they found a good place to live. Their life was very different from that of the Paleo-Indians and the Archaic peoples.

Early Spanish explorers named this area. Father Escalante, a Catholic priest, and his exploring party had camped near the north end of the present Mesa Verde park on August 11, 1776. On November 19, 1829, Antonio Armijo's expedition camped on the Mancos River at the southeast edge of the mesa. Both men left records of their trips, but neither of them spent much time in the area. It was the Spanish, however, who named the land *Mesa Verde*, or "Green Tableland."

Mesa Verde Cliff Dwellings as they appear today.

Discoveries and Pot Hunters

It was a long time before Americans were to discover the cliff dwellings that were built in the sheltering caves of the sharp cliffs. But, finally, William H. Jackson, an early photographer of the West, heard rumors about the caves and set out to find them in 1874. He did discover and photograph a small ruin which he called "Two Story Cliff House." The next year a government survey party found another ruin which they named "Sixteen Window House."

By this time ranchers were beginning to settle near the Mesa Verde, and most of them seemed to know of the many cliff dwellings in the Mesa Verde and the surrounding area. In 1886, a young writer, Virginia Donahe McClurg, visited the Ben K. Wetherill homestead. She was excited by the large collection of prehistoric artifacts gathered from the area by the five Wetherill sons. She equipped her own expedition and set out to find some sites. During a two-week period she found three rather large sites, "Three-tiered House," "Echo Cliff House," and "Balcony House."

But the largest of all the cliff dwellings was not discovered until 1888. Richard Wetherill and his brother-in-law, Charlie Mason, spent much of their time riding herd on the cattle owned by Richard's father. They always kept their eyes open in the hope of finding more ruins. Their friend, Acowitz, a Ute Indian, had told them of a "big house" hidden in a huge cave in one of the canyons. On a cold December day, as they were looking for lost cattle, they came to the rim of Cliff Canyon. Across the canyon they saw a huge cave with an enormous ruined city under the sheltering rock. They named the city "Cliff Palace." Later that same day they saw another large cliff dwelling which they called "Spruce Tree Ruin." The next day they discovered "Square Tower Ruin."

Then they hurried back to the ranch to outfit themselves to return to dig among the ruins. During the first excavation they found baskets, mummies, tools, weapons, and some of the beautiful black-and-white Mesa Verde pottery. They kept records about what they dug up, but when word got around that the Wetherills were paid $3,000 for part of their collection, other, less careful, men began to dig in the ruins.

No one can blame the cowboys and miners of the region for their years of destructive "pot-hunting." People then did not know that they were destroying valuable scientific information. But by 1893, many people began to think that something of importance to everyone was being ruined at Mesa Verde. Some heard about the ruins because they attended the World's Columbian Exposition that year. There they saw a great collection of artifacts gathered by the Wetherill family, and they were amazed by this glimpse into the life of a people from the past. Others heard about the scientific expedition to Mesa Verde by a Swedish scientist, Gustaf Nordenskiold. He described his excavations in a well-illustrated book, *The Cliff Dwellers of Mesa Verde*.

In 1900, the Colorado Cliff Dwellings Association was formed by a group of the state's women. They wrote about the ruins and gave lectures all over the country. They made an agreement with the Utes to enter the land legally and take steps to protect the ruins. Before this time Mesa Verde had been part of the Ute Reservation and pot hunters had been trespassing. Year after year bills were introduced to Congress to make the area a national park. Finally, on June 29, 1906, the Mesa Verde National Park became a reality. It was the first park established to protect the ruins of an older civilization. It was also in this year that the Federal Antiquities Act was passed. This made it a criminal offense to remove artifacts from any ruins anywhere in the country. At last, archeologists could begin putting together the story of these amazing Indians.

An example of the world-famous Mesa Verde pottery.

DID YOU KNOW?

- Dogs were pets of Indians as long ago as the Basketmakers.
- Four-story "apartment" houses were built at Mesa Verde; Americans did not build larger ones until the 1870s.
- Mesa Verde people had more dental problems than you do today.
- Young Mesa Verde married couples lived with the wife's family.
- At their population peak, more Anasazi, early native Americans, lived in southwestern Colorado than the number of people who live in that area today.

Life at Mesa Verde

Sometime around A.D. 100 to A.D. 200, a group of people known as Basketmakers began to settle on the tops of the mesas. By the fourth century A.D., they were building pit houses and farming small patches of ground. They continued to hunt and gather native food plants. Slowly they began to improve their lives in a number of ways.

Their first houses were small and square. They were called pit houses because the floor was dug out several feet below the ground surface. In most cases, there was a bench that ran around the floor area. The fire was made in the center of the room, and there was usually an upright stone placed near it, which deflected the cool air away from the fire. A smaller room, usually toward the south, was used for storage of grain and other foodstuffs. Each house had a *sipapu*—a small hole in the ground which was a symbolic entrance from the lower spiritual world. Many of these homes were eventually burned, along with the tools, utensils, and other belongings of the owners. Did the people burn the houses when someone died? Some archeologists think so.

Although the people still depended on hunting for much of their food, they now became successful farmers as well. They planted corn, squash, and beans. They began to learn how to provide more water for their crops by building ditches and check dams. Eventually they were to build stone-lined lakes or reservoirs that would hold the run-off from melting snow and from the torrential downpours of rain that still occur in the region.

When the people had first come to Mesa Verde, they were so skilled at working with rushes and fibers they were able to make ropes, yucca sandals, and baskets that held water. To heat water in a basket was very difficult. One had to keep putting hot stones in the basket over and over again to keep the water hot enough to cook food. Now the people began to learn how to make pottery. Pottery vessels could be put right on the fire. This made cooking much easier. Storing grain in pottery vessels was also an improvement. Animals could not chew through the walls of the storage utensil and get at the food.

As far as we know, the Mesa Verde people were also the first people in the Colorado area who used the bow and arrow. Before this time, a spear, sometimes used with an atlatl, had been thrown at wild animals. The bow and arrow was more accurate. No one really knows who invented the bow and arrow; it has been found all over the world. Perhaps the Mesa Verde people learned about it from a nomadic group that came through their land.

These Basketmakers also domesticated the wild turkey. Perhaps they used these birds for food. We do know they used the feathers to make blankets or robes. A few clay pipes have been found near the pit houses. Some sort of native tobacco was probably smoked in these "cloud-blowers" for use in various ceremonies.

Trade early became important to the Mesa Verde people. Many ornaments made of shell from the Gulf of California have been found near their houses. The people were becoming richer. By A.D. 1200, they had built larger, more comfortable houses. Many times these were joined together to form a new kind of house, a *pueblo*. Many families would live in the pueblo. But the people did not give up the pit houses entirely. Instead, they dug them deeper and used these underground structures for ceremonial purposes. Some of these appear as early as the eighth century A.D. Archeologists call these pit houses *kivas*, a Hopi word for their similar ceremonial chambers.

Trash piles were always a feature of these pueblos. They were always located to the southeast of the houses and the kivas. Ordinary waste products typical of any household found their way to these large mounded trash heaps, but they were also used as a place to bury the dead. Bodies were placed in a flexed position—legs were drawn up and the arms were tied to the body. No one knows why this was done.

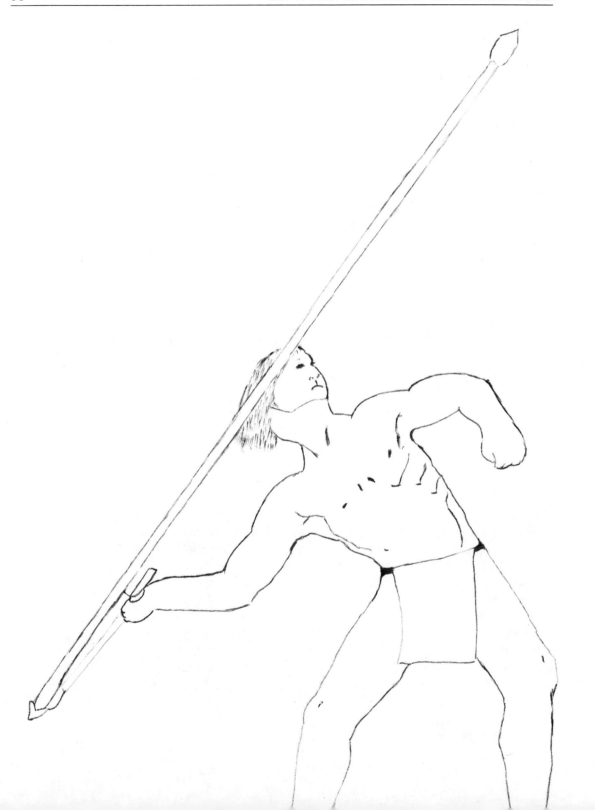

The End of an Era

Sometime soon after A.D. 1200, there was a hurried move from the "apartment" houses on the top of the mesas to the caves on the canyon walls. Although the new houses the people built were in the same style as the pueblos above, they were not as carefully constructed. Perhaps there were raids on the Mesa Verde people from newcomers to the region, and they had to build these new homes quickly.

Whatever the problem was, the people continued life much as they had done before. They kept the kivas as an important part of every village. They built towers as they had begun to do before the move. They continued to improve their farming techniques as they maintained the garden plots on the mesa tops. They also continued to improve the beautiful black-and-white pottery so appreciated today.

But the cliff dwellings were soon to be abandoned. By A.D. 1300, the people seem to have left the region. No one really knows what happened. There was a serious drought from A.D. 1276 to A.D. 1300, but there had been other droughts nearly as serious several times before. The towers suggest that there may have been an increasing number of raids on the people from outside tribes. When the first pot hunters entered the area, they found a few skeletons, but not enough to make war a strong possibility. Perhaps these were the remains of a few old and sick people who decided not to migrate with the rest of the group.

Most archeologists believe that because of overcrowding and the lack of arable farm land, the people moved to the south and settled among the Rio Grande and desert pueblo peoples. Perhaps the drought and the increasing pressure from other Indians in the area made the people simply decide that life would be better farther to the south. Whatever the reasons, the remarkable civilization they left behind is of interest to scholars and tourists alike. A trip to Mesa Verde is like a trip back in time.

An atlatl acted as an extension of the arm. It gave more force to the spear, making it go greater distances.

QUESTIONS:

1. Why do archeologists use the names of tools to identify early peoples?
2. Why should the dry climate period have changed the way people made a living?
3. Why might the Plainview people have hunted buffalo in the manner described by Joe Ben Wheat?
4. Dipper Gap was named for a topographical feature. Why might that be?
5. What is the basis for the name "Mesa Verde?"
6. What is the reason the Federal Antiquities Act was passed by the Congress?
7. Describe the ways of life of the Basketmakers.
8. What changes occurred at Mesa Verde about A.D. 1200?
9. Why did the people of Mesa Verde move away? Where might they have gone?

ACTIVITIES:

1. See if you can obtain some books about Mesa Verde. Study the photographs and other illustrations; draw or paint pictures of some of the artifacts, and then make a collage that depicts everyday life as it might have appeared about A.D. 1200.
2. Pretend that you have found a potsherd (a bit of pottery) in the school athletic field. Using some of the books listed below for information, write up a plan for the dig that you and the archeologists you have called would conduct. What equipment would you need? How would you make sure that all of the artifacts could be preserved?
3. Read one of the many good books about Mesa Verde and make a report to your class, or write a skit that you perform for the class.

Books you might enjoy:

Mary Elting and Franklin Folsom. *The Story of Archeology in the Americas*. Irving-on-Hudson, New York: Harvey House, 1960. Archeologists have developed new methods and theories since this book was written, but this is still an excellent introduction to the way archeologists work.

Franklin Folsom. *America's First Treasures*. New York: Rand McNally & Company, 1974. This is a guide to archeological sites all over the country. The section on Mesa Verde is especially good. Other parts of the book describe Folsom, Plainview, and Archaic peoples.

Deric Nusbaum. *Deric in Mesa Verde*. New York: Lippincott, 1926. This book is out of print, but it may still be found in some libraries. Deric wanders through Mesa Verde Park and day-dreams about what daily life was like when the area was alive with the early peoples.

Don Watson. *Indians of the Mesa Verde*. Mesa Verde National Park, 1961. Watson describes the artifacts found at Mesa Verde as well as how the people might have lived during the four seasons of the year. This book has become the standard reference to the Park.

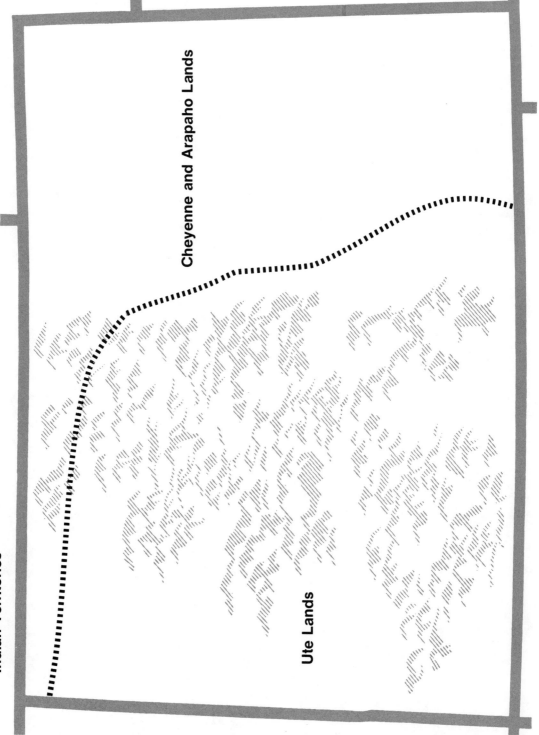

COLORADO
Indian Territories

Cheyenne and Arapaho Lands

Ute Lands

—3—

The Utes and the Plains Indians

Once an old Ute man was describing his people's history to an anthropologist. He ended his story by saying:

Then the people moved to a new site. Those camps and that life has gone now. Everything moves on and is lost. That is why the Ute say: 'It is bad luck to plan ahead.' For nothing can stop. Nothing is left of those old days but my story and your words. Nothing remains behind.

This Ute might have been speaking for all the native Americans who once called present-day Colorado their home. The Utes may have lived here for some fifteen hundred years before the Spanish described meeting with them. The Cheyenne, Arapaho, Kiowa, Comanche, Apache, Sioux, and Pawnee had been here for a century or less. But for all of these people it was bad luck to plan ahead.

The Utes

Little is known of early Ute culture. Their own oral traditions tell us that they were a small group of people who lived by stalking small animals and by food gathering. Because the land could not support a large number of people, the Utes lived in extended families rather than tribes. There were bands, seven of them, but these larger groups of related people usually

A camp of the type used by the early Ute Indians
—SHSC

gathered only in the spring for the annual Bear Dance. The rest of the time these families would go their own ways to the mountains in the summer and to the high plateaus in the winter.

Typically, the family included a man, his wife, their married sons or daughters, their own younger sons and daughters and the grandchildren. Sometimes there would also be an old widowed sister of the wife, or a brother of the husband and his family. Before the days of the horse it was hard to find enough food for even this many people.

Ute men spent most of their time hunting and fishing. They would stalk rabbit, antelope, and sometimes deer and elk. They would also clear land for the camp, butcher the meat, make the fires, and make the bows, arrows, and shields they used. Women would haul wood and water to the campsite, make and repair clothing, tan hides and dry meat, make baskets, wooden cups, and ladles, pitch the tipis or brush-covered summer lodges, gather wild berries and nuts, and do the cooking. Older children or grandparents usually cared for the younger children. The mothers were much too busy. Since age was respected, the children would often pay much more attention to their grandparents or great uncles and aunts than to their own parents. Old people were very wise. Grandfather knew where the antelope trails were, where the fish would first appear in the spring; grandmother had spent many years picking the chokecherries on the mountain slopes and knew just when and where they would first ripen. Old people also knew the proper ceremonies needed to keep the people living correctly so that the game animals would come and the wild plants would continue to bear.

The children had the happiest lives. They were greatly loved. They were considered so important that the Utes had separate

A Ute mother and her well-cared-for baby.
—SHSC

terms for newborn infants, small babies, little children, and older children, but only one word that meant adolescent and one word that meant adult. Children were never spanked or harshly punished. A scolding was usually the worst treatment a child would receive. But the easy life did not last. Before they reached their teens, Ute children were hard at work doing the routine tasks expected of a person of their sex. And the hard work was part of a generally hard life spent mostly in trying to find enough food to survive.

Only once a year, as the family left the winter camps, was there a holiday event. When the first spring thunder was heard, usually in mid-March, the Bear Dance was held. Then, a number of families from several bands would come together for several days. An old Ute man once explained:

> When bear wakes up, he's weak, he needs food, and he doesn't see well. But when they hold the dance, it helps him get out, because the helpers say to the dancers, "Get out and dance, you, because bear is waking up and that woman wants you to dance with her." It's for a good time, but it helps bears, too.

Modern Utes ready to perform the Bear Dance.
—SHSC

The dance went on for several days, and it was followed by a great feast. It was a good time to see friends, catch up on the news from other bands, and for the young people, it was a time for courtship. After the Bear Dance, there was sometimes also a Round Dance designed to drive out illness in the nearby camps or to insure health for the following year. This ceremonial gathering was one of the few things that did not change after the Utes met the whites.

The Horse Changed Everything

For generations the Utes had traded with the Pueblo Indians of Northern New Mexico. They made trips to Taos and Abiquiu to exchange furs and hides for agricultural products. But the trade was small. The Utes had little that the Pueblos wanted. The situation was the same when the Spanish occupied these northern reaches of their American empire. The Utes still had a surplus of furs and hides for trade, but the Spanish were not interested in such poor merchandise. What they did need were herdsmen for their great flocks of sheep and herds of cattle and horses. Frequently, the Spanish would capture and enslave Indian youths to do this work. They also captured or bought young Indian girls who could be trained to do the endless housekeeping chores.

Although the Utes loved their children very much, they began to sell them to the Spanish in exchange for horses. And horses made all the difference for the Utes. No longer were they dependent on the food they could obtain from their immediate environment. With horses, and later with guns, they could ride out on the plains to find the great buffalo herds. Also, with horses they could make raids on other Indian groups to steal more horses and to take captives which they could sell to the Spanish instead of their own children. Sometimes Ute children ran away from their Spanish masters and returned to their families. They often brought with them a number of horses they had stolen, and more important, they brought back the knowledge of how to handle this strange, liberating beast.

Horses and buffalo hunting changed life for the Utes. Old ways of living were discarded; new traditions developed. They still lived in small family groups during part of the year, but during late summer when the buffalo gathered into large herds for mating, the Ute bands came together for communal hunts. Great quantities of meat and hides were easily carried on the

*Buffalo meat was hung to dry
for later use.
—SHSC*

backs of horses to the central camps. There meat was dried for
use during the seasons when the buffalo were less abundant;
there tipi covers, shirts, dresses, leggings, moccasins, skin bags,
buffalo robes, shields, quivers, bowstrings, and dozens of other
items were made.

More Changes

Such an enormous change in the economic base, or way of
making a living, brought other changes. Organized buffalo
hunts and raids on other tribes to maintain or increase the
horse herds required strong leaders. Also, now that so many
families were camping near each other throughout much of
the year there was more potential for conflict. Accordingly,
strong men began to emerge as camp leaders, as leaders of the
hunt, or as leaders in warfare. But warfare was never conducted
among the Utes merely for glory as it was among many of the
Plains Indians. Their main interest in going to war was to
obtain plunder. They always shared horses just as they had
always shared meat from the hunt. A Ute chief explains why
being generous was so important:

> After a raid, the Ute gave away the horses they didn't need.
> The warriors gave them away to people who wanted them.
> But if a man was poor, he could trade those horses for some-

thing he needed—buckskin or meat. They gave away buffalo meat the same way when they came back from the hunt. Anyone could send a child over for fresh meat. The child came over to the camp when they brought the meat in, and just sat there, waiting. Never say a word. Everyone knew what the child was sent for. In the band camp, you were expected to give a present when it was needed. Some day the other family would help you out. Captured horses were the same. A man would be wanted for chief if he gave away horses to all those poor people.

Women maintained their important role in the society. During warfare they normally stayed a safe distance away with the camp equipment packed and ready for the ride to safety. However, when raids were made on their own lands, they too went into battle. They were armed and they wore full battle regalia, including headdresses. Their main job was to scalp fallen enemies and to strip them of any useful possessions.

Those women took part in the war dance which always followed successful battles. They danced, just as the men did, but their steps were those of a lame person. This was to show the difficulty they had had in carrying back the plunder acquired. All such possessions were shared with the whole band, with the exception of the scalps taken. These were sewed to the shirts of the men who had killed the enemy.

As time went on, the Utes began to adopt some of the traditions of the Plains Indians, but they chose only those items of culture that fit their existing society. While many of the Plains tribes had as many as six to ten military societies, the Utes had only one. This camp society was composed of young men who were orphans, captives of other tribes, or recruits. They lived off from the main camp a bit and spent their time in military training. This group was called the *sari'dzka*, or Dogs. They were led by a few older men who saw to their training, and one old woman, *Bi'a*, or Mother, who cooked for them and delivered their messages to the main camp. These young men were responsible for keeping a constant lookout for enemies and for guarding the people as they moved. When times were peaceful they would often serenade the camp from a distance, and they were often the ones to organize social dances.

The Utes also began to perform the Sun Dance. Among the Arapaho and the Cheyenne, this was a ceremony that involved great self torture, a sacrifice of self to bring good fortune, or

This photograph of a Ute camp was taken in 1874 by William H. Jackson, one of the great photographers of the west. —SHSC

to prevent bad fortune. Typically, near the conclusion of several days of activity, the young men would have skewers of wood thrust into flaps of skin cut on their chest. The skewers would be tied to a central pole in a large lodge. The men would strain against the rope for a determined length of time or until the skin was pulled from their bodies and they were freed. The Utes did not carry the dance to that extreme. They felt that the purpose of the dance was to obtain power for the good of the people, not to torture themselves. But power for the good of the people was not going to last.

The Utes had adapted to the challenges of the horse, the gun, and warfare with the Plains Indians. However, for them, it remained bad luck to plan ahead.

DID YOU KNOW?

- The Utes brewed spearmint tea and drank it to cure an upset stomach.
- A popular Ute game was shinny, like present-day lacrosse.
- The Ute Bear Dance usually lasted for three days and three nights.
- Utes believed whistling at night might cause the coyote to attack.

Horsemen of the Plains

Of all the Indians who had lived on the plains of what is now Colorado, the Cheyenne and the Arapaho made the most lasting impression. Like the Utes, these people had a strong sense of loyalty to their tribes. Both had lived far to the north before the eighteenth century. Both tribes had separated into a northern and a southern band. An Arapaho describes how that happened:

> We originated in the north beyond the Missouri River, and we became separated by the breaking up of the ice on the Missouri River—that is the way we left some of our people up there. After we came south to the Black Hills we separated again because the Northern Arapaho preferred to stay north and we preferred to come south. We did not do it on account of any quarrel or unpleasantness; we came south because there were more horses and a milder climate. . . . We have since lived with the Southern Cheyenne. Our Sun Dance is like theirs, but is held separately.

Much of the Arapaho life was like the Cheyenne, but held separately. The two tribes did frequently act together in making war, and sometimes they combined for the hunt. Both groups had soldier societies, and both had leaders for war and leaders for peace. They reared their children in very nearly the same manner, and sometimes they intermarried. They remained close friends all through the time that they lived on the plains.

Like the Utes, the Plains Indians found that the horse made all the difference. It made it easier to obtain the buffalo that provided food and tools and it made warfare a glorious challenge. Rigid rules were developed to ensure proper behavior. George Bird Grinnell, a close observer of the Cheyenne, describes some of these rules in his book, *When Buffalo Ran*. In it, the main character, Wikis, describes his life:

> I must have been ten years old when my uncle first began to talk to me. . . . All my life I have tried to remember what he told me this first time that he talked with me, for it was good advice, and it came to me from a good man, who afterwards became one of the chiefs of the tribe.

Wikis' uncle explained that a youth must always listen when adults spoke and must do whatever he was told. "Do not wait; do not make anyone speak to you a second time; start at once." He also told Wikis that a good man was up at dawn and looked

A busy Cheyenne Indian camp.
—SHSC

to his horses the first thing. Weapons had to be kept in good order. "But there is one thing more important than anything else, and that is to be brave." A good man, he said, would always be in front of the fighting and try hard to strike many of the enemy. Finally, he told Wikis, one must never brag. "If you should chance to perform any brave act, do not speak of it; let your comrades do this; it is not for you to tell of the things that you have done."

At thirteen Wikis went on his first buffalo hunt, and at fifteen he was allowed to go to war for the first time. Although he was unsure of himself, he did well, stealing a bow case and a quiver full of arrows from an unoccupied enemy lodge and stealing one horse from the enemy herd.

For a time, life was good for Wikis and his tribe. Buffalo were plentiful, and the Cheyenne continued to be lucky in war. But the events that were to mark the end of traditional Plains culture were near at hand. Wikis describes what it was like:

It was but a few years after I took Standing Alone for my wife, when my oldest boy was four years old, that the wars were begun between the white people and my tribe. This was a hard time. It is true we killed many people and captured much property, but . . . my uncle and I felt that the Indians were being crowded out, pushed further and further away from where we had always been—where we belonged. After each expedition through the country by white troops and after each fight . . . we felt as if some great hand was all around my tribe . . . and that at last it would grasp us and squeeze it to death. Of that bad time and of what followed that time, I do not wish to speak, and so my story ends.

A camp much like the one Wikis might have lived in. —National Archives

QUESTIONS:

1. How did the acquisition of the horse change the way of life of the Utes?

2. The Utes often gave away the horses they captured in a raid. What does that tell you about their value system? Explain.

3. Describe the role of women in Ute society.

4. How were the Utes affected by their knowledge of the Plains tribes?

5. How did the Arapaho happen to come to Colorado?

6. Why were the Arapaho and the Cheyenne such good friends?

7. What was the "great hand" that Wikis feared? Was his fear justified?

ACTIVITIES:

1. Draw a map on which you label the territories of the various Indian groups that once lived in Colorado. Make small sketches on the map that will show how these groups lived.

2. How were the youth of the Utes and the Cheyennes alike? How were they different? Explain these differences by writing diary entries as if you were a young Ute and a young Cheyenne.

3. Use an encyclopedia to learn about the buffalo, or bison, that once ranged all over Colorado. Make a report to the class so that they will better understand the importance of the buffalo to the native American way of life.

4. Read Grinnell's *When Buffalo Ran* and either write a book report or write a series of one-act plays that could be performed by the class so that you will all gain a better understanding of Cheyenne life.

Books you might enjoy:

George Bird Grinnell. *When Buffalo Ran*. New Haven: Yale Univer-
     sity Press, 1920. This may be a difficult book to find as it is
     so old. It is, however, a classic book about what it was like
     to be a Plains Indian before and immediately following white
     contact. It is written as a novel, but it is accurate in its portrayal
     of Wikis' life.

George Bird Grinnell. *The Fighting Cheyenne*. Norman: University
     of Oklahoma Press, 1956. Grinnell was an expert on the early
     life of the Cheyenne. This is a somewhat difficult book, but
     one that is exciting to read.

Virginia Cole Trenholm. *The Arapahoes, Our People*. Norman: Uni-
     versity of Oklahoma Press, 1970. Another difficult but re-
     warding book. Ms. Trenholm did the research on the Arapaho
     for James Michener as he prepared *Centennial*, his exciting
     novel about Colorado.

Edwin Tunis. *Indians*. New York: Thomas Y. Crowell, Revised edi-
     tion, 1979. This is a good overview of Indians in America.
     It is mostly about pre-white contact.

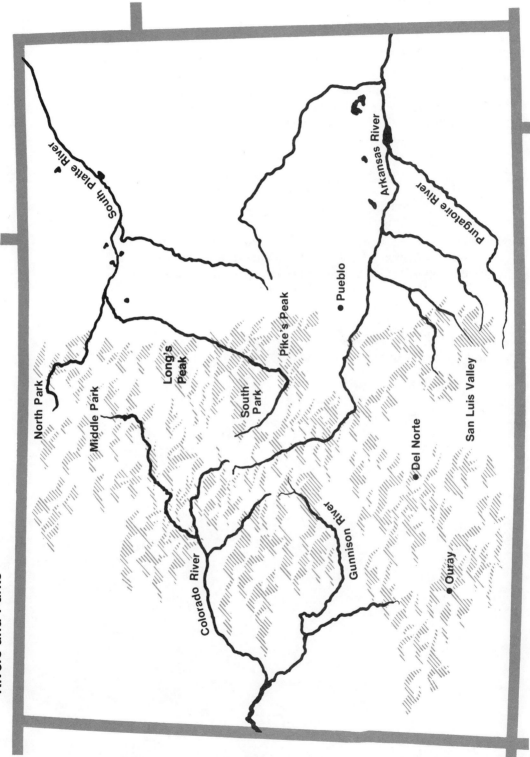

COLORADO
Rivers and Parks

South Platte River

Arkansas River

Purgatoire River

Pueblo

Pike's Peak

Long's Peak

North Park

Middle Park

South Park

Del Norte

San Luis Valley

Colorado River

Gunnison River

Ouray

—4—
Trailmarkers and Fur Trappers

Long before Wikis had come into contact with Americans from the East, there had been Europeans who had turned their eyes toward the land of present-day Colorado. The Spanish had discovered, conquered, and claimed as their property the "New World" of America. They were particularly interested in the land that lay west of the Mississippi River. Moving north from Mexico in the early seventeenth century, they had attempted to find the famous seven cities of gold that the shipwrecked Cabeza de Vaca had been told about by the native Americans on the Texas coast. Several expeditions had been sent out to find these cities, but none of the early explorers are known to have touched upon this state. However, between the mid-seventeenth century and the late eighteenth century, a number of Spanish expeditions did enter Colorado.

The Trailmarkers: The Spanish

The first European group that we are certain came to this land was led by Juan Archuleta, who set out to capture Indians who had fled from Spanish rule. This took place in 1650. Other expeditions came to Colorado for the same reason. Their purpose was not to explore, but all the same, they charted the land as they traveled through it. For example, in 1706 Juan

Ulibarri traveled from Taos, New Mexico, to an area near present-day Pueblo, Colorado, turned east, captured runaway Indians and returned to Taos. His trip was especially important because he claimed the land for the king of Spain, and because he named the area he had been in the "San Luis Valley." Several similar expeditions took place in the years that followed. By 1776, the map of Colorado was dotted with Spanish names: Los Pinos, Sangre de Cristo, La Plata and Rio Grande.

It was in 1776 that the famous Dominguez-Escalante expedition set forth to try to discover an overland route from New Mexico to California. These Spanish priests, along with eight other men, found the first part of their trip easy. Trails had already been mapped by earlier expeditions. They entered Colorado near the site of Pagosa Junction, crossed a number of well-known rivers, and then turned northward to the Rio Do-

Escalante's route through Colorado.

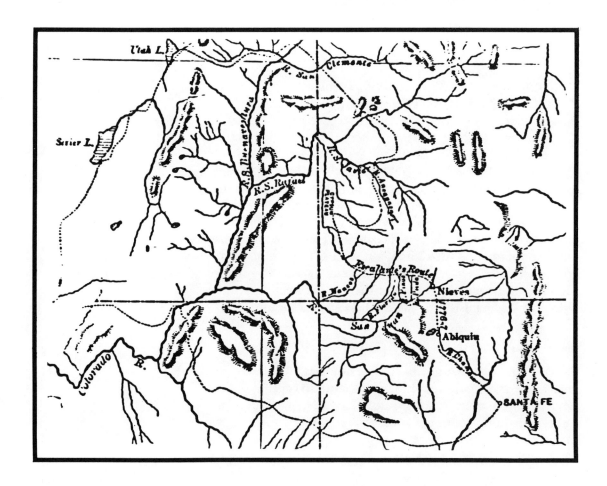

lores. Here their knowledge and their luck ran out. They found the land difficult to traverse. They turned eastward in the hope of finding an Indian who could guide them. Finally, they crossed the Uncompahgre Plateau and Father Escalante wrote in his diary:

> We entered the pleasant valley of the River of San Francisco called by the Yutahs the Ancapagari, which the interpreter tells us means Colorado Lake, from the fact that near its source there is a spring of reddish water, hot and disagreeable to the taste.

These were the famous hot springs near Ouray, Colorado. Following the Gunnison River to Grand Mesa and then to the White River, the men found their way to Utah, where they gave up their attempt to reach California. They headed south and eventually made their way back to Santa Fe. In one sense their trip was a failure; they had failed to find the route to California. In another sense, however, the trip was a success. They had penetrated a large section of unexplored land and had carefully charted and mapped it. So complete, in fact, was Father Escalante's diary that two hundred years later, in celebration of the Bicentennial, the Escalante-Dominguez Trail was marked and opened to hardy hikers.

The Trailmarkers: The Americans

Even as the Spanish were making expeditions into the Southwest, there were many Americans in the British colonies in eastern America who were speculating upon what lay beyond the Mississippi River. Young Thomas Jefferson was wildly curious. French fur trappers had told him there were "great supplies of furs and peltry" that could be bought from the Native Americans. But just as interesting to Jefferson were the stories of great mountains and valleys of unbelievable beauty. He wanted to know all about the Native American tribes who lived there, and he was equally curious about the plants and animals that were supposed to be so different from those he saw around him in Virginia.

When he became president, Jefferson negotiated the Louisiana Purchase. As quickly as possible he sent explorers to find out the truth about this vast new American territory. First he sent Lewis and Clark on their famous trip to the Pacific Northwest. Then he sent Lieutenant Zebulon Pike to find the

Pike depicted as heroic soldier and explorer.
—*SHSC*

source of the Mississippi River. Finally, in 1806 he sent Pike and some other soldiers to examine the "Head Branches of the Arkansaw and Red Rivers." It was this expedition that began the American efforts to map the land that was to become Colorado.

Pike had been charged by the government to: observe the geography, natural history, and topography of the area visited; collect mineral and botanical samples; arrive at an agreement with the Comanches; and, when he reached the Arkansas River, to split his command into two groups—one to follow that river to its mouth, the other to discover its source. Pike himself led the group that went up the Arkansas.

It was in mid-November that he made the most famous of his journal entries:

> Saturday. 15th November . . . . At two o'clock in the afternoon, I thought I could distinguish a mountain to our right, which appeared like a small blue cloud; viewed it with my spy glass, and was still more confirmed in my conjecture, yet only communicated it to Doctor Robinson . . . but in half an hour it appeared in full view before us. When our small party arrived on the hill, they with one accord gave three *cheers* to the *Mexican* mountains.

After Pike gave up his attempt to climb the peak that later bore his name, he wandered around a bit and finally ended up in the cold, wintry San Luis Valley. Although he apparently did not realize he was in Spanish territory, the Spanish themselves were well aware. He was arrested by Spanish troops and sent to New Mexico and then to Chihuahua in old Mexico for questioning. He was finally released and he reentered the United States in 1807. Pike, the explorer, had failed to find the source of the Arkansas and the Red rivers, and he had allowed himself to be captured by enemy soldiers. He even earned the nickname, "the Lost Pathfinder," but his expedition was not a complete failure.

He took back much valuable information about the geography and the natural resources of Colorado. Even though many of his papers had been taken from him, he was still able to publish a record of what he had seen and done. That record, the *Arkansaw Journal*, was popular reading in the United States and in Europe as well. Promoted to General, Pike was to die during the War of 1812 as he led a successful charge on York (now Toronto), Canada.

Because of the war, the government did not immediately follow up on the discoveries made by Pike. But in 1820 Stephen H. Long was sent out to find more information. His journey was a pleasant summer outing compared to Pike's difficult trip. Following the Platte River in good weather, his group was often able to make twenty-five miles a day. Although this trip provided a good deal of cartographic information, and was a help to later expeditions, it seemed to be chiefly remembered by the public for some inconsequential reasons: his companion, Dr. Edwin James, climbed Pike's Peak and collected the lovely wild blue columbine that was to become the state flower. The group spotted the famous "Two-ears Peak" that was to become known as Long's Peak. Perhaps the most lasting result of his trip was that he wrote, "Great American Desert" across his map of the high plains area. This retarded settlement in the area for a long time.

There were other government expeditions into the area. Both Colonel Henry Dodge in 1835 and Colonel Stephen Kearney in 1845 followed the route of Long as they swept through the region to hold council with the Indians. John C. Fremont came several times. He visited Ft. St. Vrain on the South Platte River, explored or visited North, Middle, and South parks, ascended the Arkansas to its source near Leadville, and barely survived a blizzard in the mountains north of Del Norte. All of his 100 pack mules froze to death, and eleven of his men perished. Later, Fremont did manage to cross Colorado's high mountain ranges while he was looking for a good route for a railroad.

The same year as Fremont's last trip, 1853, Captain John W. Gunnison led an official railroad survey. His party went up the Arkansas and the Huerfano, crossed the divide at Cochetopa Pass and descended a stream on the Western Slope, then continued on the Gunnison River to Utah where Gunnison was ambushed and killed by Indians. Both the river and the town of Gunnison were named for him.

Reading the journals of these men is quite exciting. They were self-conscious about the fact that they were the first literate people in the areas and they were careful in their descriptions. Their words were to whet the appetites of adventurous people from the East. They made traveling to the West seem a great adventure.

Major Stephen H. Long as painted in 1937 by Juan Menchaco from earlier portrait.
—SHSC

The Fur Trappers

There were other men who found the West to be a great adventure. The fur trappers are often called "pathfinders," since they followed the tracks of the native Americans as they wandered around the great expanses of the West. Few of them made maps, but they knew the land. Hiram Chittenden describes the role of pathfinding mountain men:

> It was the roving trader and the solitary trapper who first sought out these inhospitable wilds, traced the streams to their sources, scaled the mountain passes, and explored a boundless expanse of territory where the foot of the white man had never trodden before. The Far West became a field of romantic adventure, and developed a class of men who loved the wandering career of the native inhabitant rather than the toilsome lot of the industrious colonist.

Fur, which brought these men to the mountains, was more than a luxury in the eighteenth century. It was used to make the popular beaver hats and the beaver and mink coats that men and women alike were fond of wearing. But just as important were the fur robes used as bedcovers and as rugs by those who could afford them. There was no central heating in those days, and in winter the houses of northern Europe and the northeastern United States could become very cold indeed. British and French companies had made fortunes trapping the fur-bearing animals found along the streams and rivers of Lower Canada and the Great Lakes area.

Some of these British and French trappers worked their way south through the Rocky Mountains. There they were joined by American trappers. A few had been in the area before Lewis and Clark or Pike had made their journeys. In fact, Pike was to meet one of these trappers in Santa Fe. James Purcell had trapped on the South Platte and in South Park. He had also been trading with the Indians in the area. Then Purcell had wandered into Spanish territory, had been arrested and had his furs taken from him. Purcel was not discouraged however. Pike tells us that:

> He [Purcell] was once near hanged for making a few pounds of gunpowder, which he innocently did as he had been accustomed to do in Kentucky, but which is a capital crime in these provinces. He still retained the gun which he had with him . . . and said confidently that if he had two hours' start not all the province could take him.

Such self-confidence was typical. In 1811, Ezekiel Williams and nineteen other men were sent by a trading company to the headwaters of the South Platte and Arkansas rivers. They trapped and traded with the Indians, but soon Williams and two other men were taken prisoner by the Arapaho. After being held for two years, Williams finally escaped and made his way back to Missouri. Far from being discouraged by this experience, he immediately joined up with another group of trappers and headed back to the fur country.

Williams was lucky. Of 116 men known to have set out one season, only sixteen survived. When trapper Antoine Robidoux was sixty-two years old, he knew of only three other trappers of the over 300 he had personally known who were still alive. What made men like Purcell, Williams, and Robidoux play this gambling game with their lives? Some, such as Zenas Leonard of Pennsylvania, wanted to escape from the dull life of farming. When Leonard turned twenty-one, he told his father, "I can make my living without picking up stones!" He left for St. Louis, joined John Gantt's hunting party, and headed for the mountains. That first winter made him wonder if he had made a good decision. He describes what it was like in the North "park" of Colorado.

Christopher "Kit" Carson in his later years. Carson was Indian fighter, guide, scout, Army officer and farmer before his death in 1868.
—SHSC

> Here we were in a desolate wilderness, uninhabited by even the hardy savage or wild beast—surrounded on either side by huge mountains of snow, without one mouthful to eat save a few beaver skins—our eyes almost destroyed by piercing wind, and our bodies at times almost buried by the flakes of snow which were driven before it. Oh! How heartily I wished myself home.

Leonard did survive that awful winter, and he stayed in the fur trade for three more years. Then he spent the last years of his life as a farmer.

Other men, such as Kit Carson, were eager for adventure:

> I was apprenticed to David Workman to learn the saddler trade. I remained with him two years. The business did not suit me, and having heard so many tales of life in the Mountains of the West, I concluded to leave him. He was a good man, and I often recall to my mind the kind treatment I received from his hands. But taking into consideration that if I remained with him and served my apprenticeship I would have to pass my life in labor that was distasteful to me, and anxious to travel, for the purpose of seeing different countries, I concluded to join the first party for the Rocky Mts.

What Carson neglected to say was that when he "concluded to leave" Workman, he was breaking a legal contract to complete his apprenticeship.

Workman was angry that Carson had run away, but "going west" was in the air. Less than a year later, Workman himself joined Ezekiel Williams and a company of over a hundred men who were going to trade with the Mexicans in Santa Fe.

Six Dollars a Peltry

While some men joined the fur trade to escape the boredom back home and others went just for the adventure, the main reason for all of them was that fur trading could mean good money. With luck, a trapper could catch two to four hundred beaver in a season. At four to six dollars a skin, or "peltry" as they were called by the fur men, a man could earn from one to two thousand dollars a season. In those days, carpenters, masons, and other skilled workers were making $400 to $600 for a full twelve months' work.

Trapping the clever beaver was not easy. Traps were set in streams, rivers, ponds, and swamps. Beaver are nocturnal animals, so at dusk the trapper would wade upstream until he found a beaver's natural runway. He would chain each trap so that if a beaver were caught, it would be drowned. This was necessary, for if a beaver were allowed to breathe after being caught, it would chew its own leg off to escape the trap. Over each trap, the mountain man would bend a twig baited with castoreum, the beaver's own scent. At dawn, the trapper would return to his traps. He would skin the forty-pound animals on the spot and carry the hides back to camp for preparation. Rufus Sage describes how this was done:

James P. Beckwourth as a businessman after he retired from the fur trade.
—SHSC

> The usual mode of dressing skins consists of removing all fleshy particles from the pelt, and divesting it of a thin viscid substance upon the exterior, known as the 'grain'; then, after permitting it to dry, it is thoroughly soaked in a liquid decoction formed from the brains of the animal and water, when it is stoutly rubbed with the hands in order to open its pores and admit the mollient properties of the fluid,—this done, the task is completed by alternate rubbings and distensions until it is completely dry and soft.
>
> In this manner a skin may be dressed in a very short time, and, on application of smoke, will not become hardened from any subsequent contact with water.

Usually, the skins were stretched to dry on willow frames. Sometimes these frames were placed over pits that contained a smoldering fire. That would speed up the drying process. This was often necessary as the camps were moved every day or so. Trappers had to work fast to try to trap as many beaver as possible during the short season the pelts were in their best shape.

Rufus Sage had been a mountain man during the 1830s. He was well educated and he kept a journal during his time in the fur trade. When he returned to the East, he wrote a book describing his experiences. Here he describes what a typical mountain man looked like:

> His skin, from constant exposure, assumes a hue almost as dark as that of the Aborigine American Indian, and his features and physical structure attain a rough and hardy cast. His hair . . . becomes long, coarse, and bushy, and dangles upon his shoulders . . . . His clothes are of buckskin, gaily fringed at the seams with strings of the same material, cut and made in a fashion peculiar to himself . . . . His waist is encircled with a belt of leather, holding encased his butcher-knife and pistols—while from his neck is suspended a bullet pouch securely fastened to the belt in front, and beneath the right arm hangs a powder-horn transversely from his shoulder, behind which . . . are affixed his bullet-mould, ball screw, wiper, awl, &c. With a gun-stick made of some hard wood and a good rifle placed in his hands, carrying from thirty-five balls to the pound, the reader will have before him a correct likeness of a genuine mountaineer when fully equipped.

Most trappers did look just as Sage described them and as Frederick Remington and Charles M. Russell painted them. They usually had at least two horses—one to carry the mountain man, and the other to carry the extra supplies, six or seven five-pound beaver traps, the prepared beaver skins, and a buffalo robe from which the trapper made his bed.

DID YOU KNOW?

- The average beaver pelt weighed 1 1/2 pounds.
- Beaver pelts sold for $4 per pound.
- In September 1806 Pike's party averaged 19 miles a day on horseback.
- On June 30, 1820 at 11:00 A.M. the Long expedition found the temperature of the Platte River 75° and the air 80°.

Frederick Remington, noted western artist, portrayed the mountain man as grizzled, tough and independent.
—SHSC

In the early days, trappers would make their way to eastern settlements to sell their furs. Later, the fur buyers would send out wagon trains to a predetermined rendezvous site where they would buy furs from the trappers and sell them needed supplies. The rendezvous became very famous as a meeting ground for men who may not have seen many other human beings for months. There would be gambling, foot and horse races, dancing in the evenings with women from Plains tribes who also attended the affair, and much drinking of liquor. Rich at the beginning of the rendezvous from the good prices obtained for the fur pelts, many men ended the meeting completely broke. Later, when trading posts began to dot the foothills and plains, the rendezvous died out.

Finally, the fur trade itself began to die out. Silk hats rather than beaver hats became the fashion for men. Women began to find the more delicate fur of the mink and the marten more attractive than beaver. The price for pelts fell as low as $3 per pound, and it cost nearly that much to trap and market them. The mountain men began to cast around for other occupations. Some became traders. Others became Indian fighters, farmers, or hunters, while still others found jobs as guides for the great army expeditions that were being sent out by the government to map the uncharted West.

QUESTIONS:

1. Who do you think were the most important explorers of early Colorado?

2. What personal qualities did explorers need to have?

3. Why was Thomas Jefferson's interest in the West so important?

4. Explain the importance the fur trappers played in increasing people's knowledge of the West.

5. Why were beaver so important? How were they trapped and processed?

6. Why did so many young men choose such a dangerous way to make a living?

ACTIVITIES:

1. Write a series of journal accounts as if you were a member of one of the early fur trapping expeditions.

2. Prepare a talk for the class in which you describe the nature of the beaver. Use sketches you have made that will show its natural range, the dams it makes, and the appearance of the animal at different stages in its life.

3. Read one of the accounts of the fur trappers and give a more detailed account of the equipment used as well as the experiences of some of the famous trappers of Colorado.

4. Have several members of the class make short reports on the explorations of the men mentioned in this chapter, as well as other early explorers.

Books you might enjoy:

Don Berry. *Mountain Men.* Sausalito, CA: Comstock Ed., 1966.
    This book is easily read, and it gives a good picture of how
    the fur trappers lived.

Olive Burt. *Jedidiah Smith: Fur Trapper of the Old West.* New York:
    Jullian Messner, 1951. This story of one of the most famous
    mountain men tells much about their daily lives and typical
    experiences.

Harvey L. Carter. *Zebulon Montgomery Pike: Pathfinder and Patriot.*
    Colorado Springs: Denten Print Co., 1956. This is a sym-
    pathetic account of the life of Pike. Carter tries to prove that
    Pike was never the "lost pathfinder," as some other historians
    have suggested.

Lewis H. Garrard. *Wah-to-yah and the Taos Trail.* Norman: Univer-
    sity of Oklahoma Press, 1955. This book was first published
    in 1850. Garrard was seventeen years old when he went West
    in 1846. He kept a diary as he traveled, and the book was
    written from those notes. The book is a bit difficult since the
    writing style was different in his day, but it is a rewarding
    book to read as Garrard was a careful and sympathetic observer
    of the early Western frontier.

Carl P. Russell. *Firearms, Traps, and Tools of the Mountain Man.* New
    York: Knopf, 1967. This is a how-they-did-it book. It gives
    an interesting explanation of the technology available to the
    fur trappers.

Stanley Vestal. *Mountain Men.* Boston: Houghton, Mifflin, 1937.
    This old book about the mountain men makes for exciting
    reading. Some parts of it are difficult, but it is rewarding, and
    worth the effort.

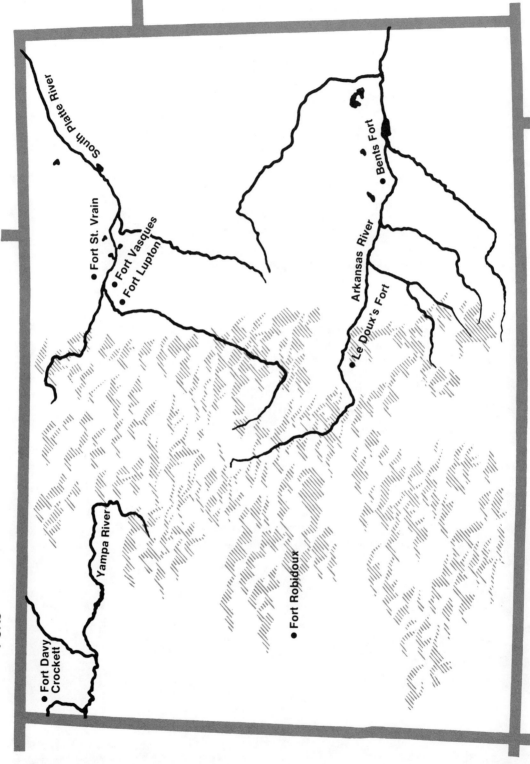

COLORADO
Forts

South Platte River

Fort St. Vrain

Fort Vasques

Fort Lupton

Bents Fort

Arkansas River

Le Doux's Fort

Yampa River

Fort Davy Crockett

Fort Robidoux

5

The Traders

The mountain men and the explorers were not the only Americans who came to Colorado in the 1820s. Others came to trade with the native Americans and with the people of northern Mexico. Under Spanish control the Santa Fe merchants had not been allowed to trade with Americans. Instead, they had to make the long journey to Chihuahua or Mexico City, where taxes were very high. After the Mexicans won their independence from Spain in 1821, the new Mexican government acted quickly to make trade with Americans legal. One of the first people to take advantage of this was William Becknell. Becknell traveled from Missouri to Santa Fe with well-loaded pack mules. On a second trip he managed to get three wagons through. Becknell not only made a lot of money from these trading trips, he also gained the nickname, "Father of Santa Fe Trade."

Soon other parties were setting out for the New Mexican capital. Several managed to get through with wagons, and by 1825 these merchants were reporting enormous profits from the trade. Trade goods brought cash payments in gold and silver, and wagons returning to Missouri carried loads of hardware and brightly colored textiles. However, raiding Indians began to be a problem for the traders. The U.S. government was asked to help. First, the trail was marked so that the wagon trains would not get lost, and then, beginning in 1829, the government began to provide military escorts.

Among the Santa Fe traders were the Bent brothers, Charles and William, and their friend Ceran St. Vrain. They were also experienced in the fur trade. In 1832, they had an idea. They thought it would be easier if they stayed in one spot and let the Indians bring furs to them in exchange for trade goods. The idea was a good one, but the location they had chosen was not. Yellow Chief, a Cheyenne friend of William Bent, suggested that the best location for a trading post would be one that was close to the buffalo hunting grounds of the Plains Indians. After a short search, the perfect location was found. It was on the Arkansas River. To the north and the west were the lands of the Cheyenne, Arapaho, and Utes. Across the river to the south were the lands of the Comanche, Kiowa, and Kiowa-Apache. The site was right on the Mountain Branch of the Santa Fe Trail, so that the fort immediately became a favorite resting place for the Bent's own wagon drivers and for those of other trading parties. Bent's Fort soon became one of the most famous trading posts in the West.

Bent's Fort: Center of an Empire

Previous forts in the West had been built as stockades. The outer walls were of heavy logs placed vertically, and the living spaces within the walls were usually simple log cabins. The Bents and St. Vrain wanted something more impressive and more practical for their great trading station. All of the men had been to Santa Fe and Taos, where they had seen massive buildings made of adobe. This was a much more useful building material in an area where wood was scarce and where the danger of Indian attacks was very real. Adobe walls could be built just as high as log ones, but they could not be set afire from the outside by Indians. Adobe buildings were also very cool in the summer and warm in the winter. The two-foot-wide walls provided excellent insulation. This was very practical in a climate that ranged from over one hundred degrees in the summer to below zero during the harsh winters. When the fort was completed, it was the largest trading post in the Southwest. It impressed everyone who saw it. Many people left sketches and written descriptions of the fort itself and of their experiences during their visits. Lewis Garrard, a seventeen-year-old, made a grand tour of the West in 1846. He described Bent's Fort this way:

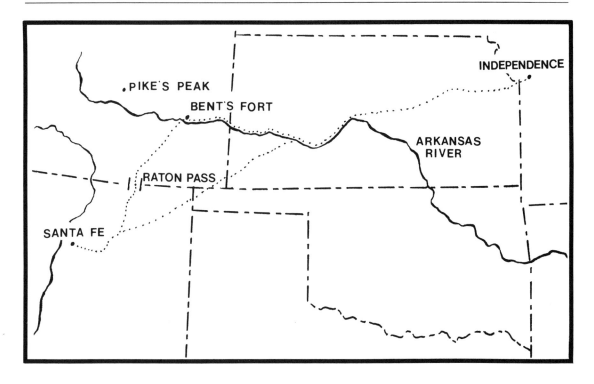

The fort is a quadrangular structure, formed of *adobes*, or sun dried brick. It is thirty feet in height and one hundred feet square. . . . The fort walls serve as the back walls to the rooms, which front inward on a courtyard. In the center of the court is the "Robe Press" [used to flatten buffalo pelts for easier shipping] and lying on the ground was a small brass cannon. . . . There was a billiard table in a small house on top of the fort . . . and in the clerk's office, contiguous, a first rate spyglass . . . . In the belfry two eagles of the American bald species, looked from their prison.

Map of the Santa Fe Trail.

Garrard was also impressed with the scenery:

I arose early in the morning, and going on top of the fort, I had a good view of the "Spanish Peaks" to the northwest, apparently fifteen miles distant—in reality *one hundred and twenty*. They were of a dull gray color; while a lower range were dazzling white, all perpetually covered with snow. To the northeast, a faint outline of a mountain was described—James' or Pike's Peak!

Another traveler, the Englishman George F.A. Ruxton, left a wonderful description of the people who could be found at the fort:

This model of Bent's Fort was made from a sketch drawn by a visiting soldier, Lt. James Abert.
—SHSC

All rooms of the fort opened onto the central plaza.
—SHSC

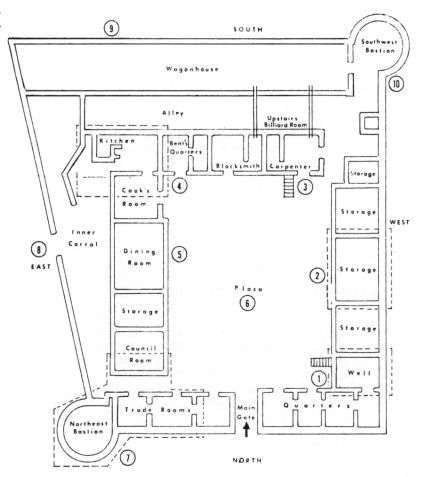

Here congregate at certain seasons the merchants of the plains and mountains, with their stocks of peltry. Chiefs of the Shian, the Kioway, and Arapaho, sit in solemn conclave with the head traders, and smoke the 'calumet' over their real and imaginary grievances . . . . In the corral, groups of leather-clad mountaineers, with 'decks' of 'euker' and 'seven-up' gamble away their hard earned peltries. The employes—mostly St. Louis Frenchmen and Canadian voyageurs—are pressing packs of buffalo skins, beating robes, or engaged in other duties of a trading fort. Indian squaws, the wives of mountaineers, strut about in all the pride of beads and fanfaron, jingling with bells and bugles, and happy as paint can make them. Hunters drop in with animals packed with deer or buffalo meat to supply the fort; Indian dogs look anxiously in at the gateway, fearing to enter and encounter the enmity of their natural enemies, the whites; and outside the fort, at any hour of the day or night, one may safely wager to see a dozen coyotes or prairie wolves loping round, or seated on their haunches, and looking gravely on, waiting patiently for some chance offal to be cast outside. Against the walls, groups of Indians, too proud to enter without an invitation, lean, wrapped in their buffalo robes, sulky, and evidently ill at ease to be so near the whites . . . their white lodges shining in the sun, at a little distance from the river-banks; their horses feeding in the plain beyond.

Even though the fort was located on the frontier, there was an attempt to live life as if the people were still all back in St. Louis. The owners, when they were present, and their guests were served meals on white tablecloths and on the best imported English china. There was a large wine cellar and on special occasions mint juleps were served with ice cut from the river in the winter and stored in an ice house near the fort. Another popular drink at the fort was hailstorms, whiskey cooled with hail stones. Evenings were frequently spent in dancing, and on some occasions the company had taffy pulls.

DID YOU KNOW:

- Oxen pulling a loaded wagon averaged twelve to fifteen miles per day.
- Mules pulling a loaded wagon averaged fifteen to twenty miles per day.
- In 1844 mules cost $100 – $200 each, oxen cost $14 each, and a wagon cost $100.

Permanent employees of the fort included blacksmiths, carpenters, wheelwrights, gunsmiths, and hunters. They came from all parts of the world and usually had Indian or Mexican wives. One visitor remarked that he "heard at one time as many as six different languages, French, Spanish, German, English, Comanche, Arapaho—a perfect Babel of a place."

Some of the most famous men of the West were employed at one time or another at the fort. These included Lucien Maxwell, who was later to own over one million acres of land in Colorado and New Mexico; Baptiste Charbonneau, son of the famous Sacajawea, who went with Lewis and Clark on their exploration of the Louisiana Territory; Kit Carson, famous trapper, army scout, guide, soldier; and Thomas Fitzpatrick, trapper, guide, and Indian agent.

For seventeen years the fort stood as a sentinel on the plains. It provided a trading station for Indians and Santa Fe traders alike. Then, events outside the control of the Bent brothers or St. Vrain began to destroy the company.

End of the Empire

When the United States annexed Texas in 1845, the Mexicans viewed the act as one of war. It soon became apparent that the United States was going to invade New Mexico, and Bent's Fort became the advance base and rendezvous for General Stephen Kearney's Army of the West. The land around the fort was overgrazed by the horses and mules of the 1,650 troopers, the 300 wagons of Santa Fe traders who were remaining behind the troops for protection, and the government wagon trains sent out to supply the armies. For a time the fort was piled up with goods and munitions, and the rooms were filled with soldiers, teamsters, and artisans. Trade was brought to a stop. Conflict between the Indians, and the soldiers and settlers heightened hostilities. Then in 1847, Charles Bent, who had been appointed governor of the newly annexed New Mexico Territory, was attacked and killed by a revolt of the Mexicans and Pueblo Indians. After the revolt was put down, St. Vrain, who sold his interest in the fort to William Bent, moved to New Mexico. William Bent maintained the trade for a while by himself, but in 1849 a cholera epidemic, brought by passing immigrants, spread through the Plains tribes. This further reduced the trade. William Bent was discouraged. The Army wanted to buy the fort, and Bent wanted to sell it.

Today, tourists enjoy these views of the reconstructed Bent's Fort.

Apparently the Army would not pay what Bent thought was a fair price. Legend says that in a burst of anger, Bent loaded up his family and his goods and drove them five miles down river. Early the next morning, he returned to the fort, set fire to the storerooms and the powder magazines and abandoned the fort.

Together with his sons and some of his employees, Bent built a second, smaller Bent's Fort thirty-eight miles away. At this second fort he reestablished the Indian trade and continued to send wagon trains to his smaller fort on the South Platte. Trade never was as good as it had been in the 1830s and 1840s, and finally, just before the Civil War, Bent retired to his farm on the upper Purgatoire River where he died in 1869.

Other Trading Posts in Colorado

Although it was the largest and best known, Bent's Fort did not stand in the wilderness alone. Maurice Le Doux ran a small post on Hardscrabble Creek near Florence in the 1830s. Fort Pueblo operated throughout the 1840s and the 1850s until it was destroyed by the Utes. Fort Uncompahgre, better known as Fort Robidoux, was located near present day Delta, and Fort Davy Crockett existed for some time at Brown's Hole on the Green River. These latter two forts were used mostly by the men who continued to trap beaver, even though the market did not really make it worthwhile any longer.

Four trading posts were built on a sixteen mile stretch of the South Platte River in the 1830s. Fort Lancaster, soon known as Fort Lupton, was one of the first to be constructed. Lieutenant Lancaster Lupton came west in 1835 when Colonel Henry Dodge was ordered to lead an expedition of his famous Dragoons (cavalry troops) on a trip to the Rocky Mountains. Lupton saw the great adobe trading post of the Bents, and noted that even though there were no posts on the Platte, the fur trade in that area was lively. As soon as the expedition returned to the East, Lupton resigned his army commission, bought a wagon load of trade goods, and returned to the West. He decided to build his small trading post on the banks of the South Platte. He used the same type of large adobe bricks from which Bent's Fort was constructed. Within three years he had three competitors. Fort Vasquez, Fort St. Vrain (a Bent and St. Vrain outpost), and Fort Jackson were all built

Fort St. Vrain as it might have appeared about 1844. From a drawing in Scribner's Magazine.

nearby. In spite of the competition, Lupton managed to make a living at his post for over ten years.

This sketch, published in Scribner's Magazine in 1876, is described as Fort Vasquez.

In trade for buffalo robes and the pelts of other animals, the Indians could obtain a variety of goods that appealed to them. A typical inventory of one of these Platte River posts included:

paper covered looking glasses . . . .@46 ¢ per dozen
finger rings . . . .@90 ¢ per gross
combs . . . .@60 ¢ per dozen
battle axes . . . .@$1.92 ½ each
powder . . . .@33 ¢ per pound
coffee . . . .@16 ½ ¢ per pound
sugar . . . .@13 ½ ¢ per pound

These prices were the ones the traders paid to their St. Louis suppliers. The Indians paid whatever the trader would dare to ask, and sometimes, when the Indians had been "softened" up with several drinks of cheap liquor, they would pay exorbitant prices. Peter Sarpy, one of the partners of Fort Jackson, admitted as much in a letter written on February 18, 1838. After describing the use of liquor, he said: "My object is to do all the harm possible to the opposition and yet without harming ourselves."

But the Indian trade began to fall off. The price of beaver pelts had been steadily declining since the silk hat became more fashionable. Buffalo robes were also in plentiful supply in the East, and the native Americans had little else to sell. Lupton decided to supplement his trade by farming and grazing. Fremont mentions the farm in his journal entry of July 6, 1843:

We reached Fort Lancaster, the trading establishment of Mr. Lupton. His post was beginning to assume the appearance of a comfortable farm; stock, hogs, and cattle, were ranging about on the prairie; there were different kinds of poultry; and there was the wreck of a promising garden, in which a considerable variety of vegetables had been in a flourishing condition, but it had been almost entirely ruined by the recent high water.

Lupton hung on for another few years, with sales to the free fur traders who often came to his fort to buy supplies or to trade their furs for supplies. One of the transactions that took place at his post was this:

Fort Lancaster, Jany. 28th 1844

Rich O. Wilson Bot. of S. Turley pr C. Orttubiz

147 lbs. flour $12 a faneaga	$14.70
One Sack corn pr Stiles	14.00
16 Galls. whiskey 4.00 pr Gall.	64.00
	$92.70
Received of L.P. Lupton 5 cows 12.00	60.00
2 steers $10.00	20.00
3 calves $4.00	12.00

In all amounting to ninety-two dollars in payment of the above.

his
CHARLES X ORTUBIZ
mark

In the summer of 1844 Lupton visited his parents in Wisconsin, and the following year he left his fort and vainly attempted to reenlist in the army. However, like most other former mountain men, he could not again fit into the established mold of society back East. He had married Thomass, the Cheyenne daughter of a chief, and had eight children by her. People in the East could not accept such a marriage. His parents' attitudes are reflected in excerpts from a letter written by his father: "You have indeed been a wanderer too long, I fear for your benefit . . . . My prayer for you dearest Lancaster, will ever be that God in his mercy may bless you with plenty and success." On the margin, his mother wrote: "I do hope *you* will come home again soon . . . you are very dear to me, Sonny." She did not ask Lancaster to bring his wife and children for a visit.

Lupton farmed for a time near Hardscrabble, but in 1849 he joined the Gold Rush to California where he remained until his death. His fort, like most of the others, was used as a camping place by the later immigrants. It was used for a while as a stagecoach station. Eventually it was destroyed as materials were taken from it to be used by homesteaders for their farm buildings.

Fort Vasquez was reconstructed in the 1930s by the Works Projects Administration as a work relief project. Unfortunately, archeologists and historians were not asked to take part in the planning, so the fort is not accurately restored. Bent's Fort, however, has been rebuilt to be as authentic as possible, and for those who wish to "feel" the atmosphere of an earlier time, a visit there is an exciting and worthwhile experience.

QUESTIONS:

1. Why was the Santa Fe trade important to the New Mexicans? The Coloradans?

2. Why did the Bents and others decide that a trading post made more sense than trade wagon trips?

3. Why was Bent's Fort built in the Mexican fashion?

4. Describe the people who could be found at Bent's Fort.

5. George F.A. Ruxton described the Indian women at Bent's Fort as "squaws," and as "happy as paint can make them." Today, such statements are considered to be racist. Why has that changed?

6. What were some of the activities that took place at Bent's Fort?

7. Why was Bent's Fort eventually abandoned?

8. Why were four trading posts built so close to each other along the Platte?

9. Why did the Indian trade begin to fall off in the 1840s?

10. Why did Lancaster Lupton finally break away from his family in Wisconsin?

11. Compare the attitudes of white Americans toward native Americans in the 1840s and today.

ACTIVITIES:

1. Pretend that you were along with seventeen-year-old Lewis Garrard on his visit to Bent's Fort. Write a letter to your family back East in which you describe the adventure.

2. Build a model of Bent's Fort. Use the materials in the text, but also check books by David Lavender and Jackson W. Moore, Jr., for more information.

3. Try to visit the site of any one of the old Colorado forts and make a report to your class about what you learned.

Books you might enjoy:

Don Berry. *A Majority of Scoundrels: An Informal History of the Rocky Mountain Fur Company*. Sausalito, CA: Comstock Ed., 1961. This is a classic book about the fur trade. Parts of it apply to the fur trappers themselves, but other sections deal with traders.

Wyatt Blassingame. *Bent's Fort: Crossroads of the Great West*. Champaign, IL: Garrard Publishing Co., 1967. An easy-to-read story of the great trading post.

David Lavender. *Bent's Fort*. New York: Doubleday, 1954. This is the classic account of the building and destruction of the fort and of all that happened in between. It is difficult reading, but absorbing if you are really interested in this topic.

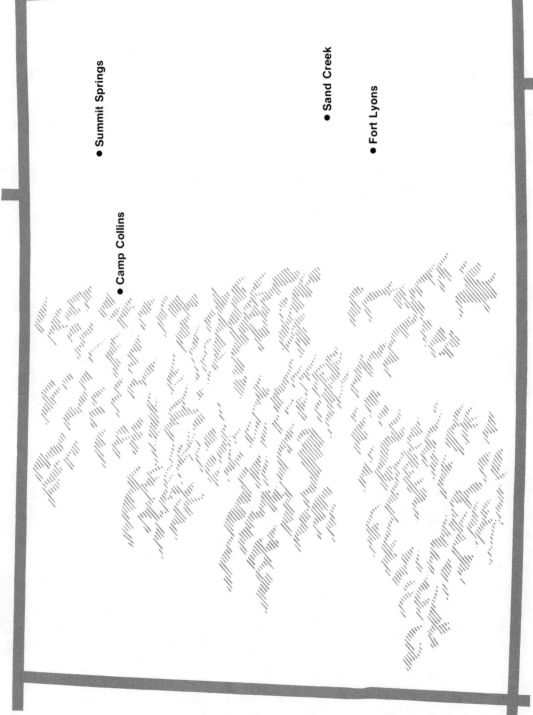

COLORADO
Battle Sites

• Summit Springs

• Sand Creek

• Fort Lyons

• Camp Collins

—6—
The Indians Must Go!

Although the Arapaho and the Cheyenne were regularly fighting with other Plains tribes, they got along fairly well with the first groups of westward moving Americans. These white men had touched the land lightly. They had trapped the beaver from the streams, but the Indian was more interested in the buffalo than the lowly beaver. White Americans had made ruts on the prairie with their wagon wheels, but wagons were few; most of the trappers and traders used pack animals just as the Indians did, and most of them followed Indian trails.

When the gold rush brought in hordes of excited Americans, the Cheyenne and Arapaho seemed more amused than frightened. For the first few years of Denver's existence, the Arapaho camped on the edge of town. In fact, they felt so comfortable, they left their women and children there when they went on raids against the Ute. But some men had foreseen a difficult future. As early as 1846, Yellow Wolf, the friend of William Bent, had told Lieutenant Abert that the Cheyenne must take up farming, or leave the country. William Bent had, of course, suggested such a plan as well. But by the time the U.S. Government was ready to act, it was too late.

The Clash of Two Cultures

The sodbusters were a main part of the problem. By plowing up and fencing in the land, they were destroying the centuries-old buffalo migration patterns. But it was not just the disruption in the food supply of the Plains people that was at the heart of the matter. What forced the open conflict was the confrontation between two incompatible cultures. "Thou shalt not steal," said the Bible of the eastern Americans. "Thou shalt

An Arapaho encampment near Denver.
—SHSC

Counting coups *or hits on an enemy showed great bravery. The* coups *stick was about 12 feet long and was decorated with feathers, bells, or brightly colored cloth.*

steal from the enemy, and it will give thee great honor," said
the code of the Plains Indians. Killing and scalping an enemy
would also bring honor, perhaps not as much as counting
coup, but it did show bravery, and being brave was the most
important thing for a man.

Still, for a time, many whites felt comfortable with their
Indian neighbors. Mrs. S.S. Sanford, a pioneer, recalled that:

> . . . one time about 700 Indians camped on our meadow.
> Each of them had two or three ponies and they would soon
> have ruined the hay. My father decided the next morning
> that he would ask them to move off. Mother objected, fearing
> that it would anger them and we might all be killed. But
> father decided to go, so, packing up some meat and other
> things to eat he went over to talk to them. He came back in
> a little while and the Indians pulled up their teepees and
> moved about a mile up the creek. After that they often came
> to our house and father treated them well. He said that no
> matter what happened he would not be afraid to go to the
> chief, Left Hand, and ask his protection.

But a visitor from the East, the famous newspaper publisher
Horace Greeley, could see trouble coming. He wrote that:

> The Arapaho chief, Left Hand, assures me that his people
> were always at war with the Utes. Some two or three hundred
> lodges of Arapahoes are encamped in and about this log city,
> calculating that the presence of whites will afford some pro-
> tection to their wives and children against a Ute onslaught
> while the braves are off on their fighting—that is, stealing—
> expeditions.

The situation, felt Greeley, could not continue as it was:

> These people must die out—there is no help for them. God
> has given this earth to those who will subdue and cultivate
> it, and it is vain to struggle against His righteous decree.

Aging William Bent agreed. For more than a year he served
as an Indian agent, and he made a strong plea for the government to take immediate action. He felt that the Indians could
indeed become farmers.

> The Cheyans and Arrapahos have took my advice to them
> last Winter and this last Spring. I am proud to say they have
> behaved themselves exceedingly well . . . . Theair will be no

troble settling them down and start farming. They tell me they . . . have passed theair laws amongst themselves thar they will do anything I may advize. It is a pitty that the Department can't send Some farming implements and other necessarys this fall Sow as they could commence farming this Coming Spring . . . . you Must excuse my bad Spelling as I have bin so long in the Wild Waste I have almost forgotten how to Spell.

Later, in an official report that was probably dictated, Bent again asked for action:

The concourse of whites is . . . constantly swelling, and incapable of control or restraint by the government. This suggests the policy of promptly rescuing the Indians and withdrawing them from contact with whites . . . . These numerous and warlike Indians, pressed upon all around by the Texans, by the settlers of the gold region, by the advancing people of Kansas, and from the Platte, are already compressed into a small circle of territory, destitute of food, and itself athwart by a constantly marching line of emigrants. A desperate war of starvation and extinction is therefore imminent and inevitable, unless prompt measures shall prevent it.

The "prompt measures" suggested by Bent were the provisions of the Treaty of Fort Wise, signed by the Cheyenne and Arapaho in February 1861, and by President Abraham Lincoln in December 1861. For a tiny patch of land along the Arkansas River, the two tribes were to give up their claim to all the land between the Arkansas and the Platte. They were to receive $450,000 for this, as well as a sawmill, grinding mills for grain, and a mechanic's shop. From the money paid to them, they were to buy agricultural tools, build houses, and fence the land. All whites were to stay off this land, except for government officials, traders, and the half-Indian men, Robert Bent, son of William Bent, and Jack Smith, son of one of Bent's important traders, who were each given 640 acres of land.

Trouble Begins

Things might have worked out. Black Kettle, a leader of the Cheyennes, was confident he would be able to get the other leaders to sign. The new Indian agent, Albert Boone, grandson of Daniel Boone, was certain he could deliver the government promises. But a peaceful solution to the problem was not to be. The Civil War began. Troopers were pulled from Colorado to fight in the East. The Cheyenne Dog Soldiers refused to sign the Treaty of Fort Wise, knowing that it could not be enforced. They, along with warriors from other tribes, renewed attacks on their Indian enemies and also began to attack the settlers.

Reports of these attacks poured in to government officials and to newspapers:

Daily and hourly I am receiving complaints of burning ranches, killing stock as well as many outrages of the gravest character perpetrated on white women.

. . . a bunch of Indians came to this ranch [near Kuner] when William Brush was there with a couple of cowboys. They acted friendly and asked Brush to shoe one of their horses. He started to do this and as he stooped over with his back turned they shot him. When the cowboys came to the door they were shot also. The Indians then went on up the Platte to Fort Latham. There they stole a horse from Baily and two from us. From there they went on to the mouth of the Thompson where Ashcraft had a ranch . . . . The Indians were followed down the Platte to a large grove of cottonwoods. The men did not dare go into the woods so came back. They were probably never caught unless they were with the band that Chivington killed later.

On July 15, 1864, the inhabitants of Denver and vicinity were shocked by the news that the Hungate family, living about thirty miles southeast of Denver, had been murdered by Indians.

Two days after the Hungate massacre, just as the home guard were disbanding from drilling on East Fourteenth Street, a man on a foaming steed galloped through our streets crying, "Indians are coming; Indians are advancing on the town to burn and massacre. Hurry your wives and children to places of safety!" Following close after this rider came men, women and children, in wagons, ox carts, on horseback and on foot, all pale with fear. The news swept over the town like the wind. Women and children of East Denver were hurried to the mint; those of West Denver to the upper story of the Commissary building on Ferry Street. No Indians appeared . . . .

But the fear remained. Newspapers demanded that action be taken against the Indians. Governor Evans wanted a war with them so he could clear them from the land. He begged for help from the War Department.

It wasn't that Evans hadn't tried to solve the problem with the resources of the territory—and Colorado had become a territory in 1861. First, he had issued a call for all peaceful Indians to gather at either Fort Lyons on the Arkansas or Camp Collins on the Cache la Poudre. He warned that those who did not obey this order would be considered as "hostiles," and were subject to attack. To the white people in the area he issued the following statement:

> Now, therefore, I, John Evans, Governor of Colorado Territory, do issue this, my proclamation, authorizing all citizens of Colorado, either individually or in such parties as they may organize, to go in pursuit of all hostile Indians on the plains, scrupulously avoiding those who have responded to my call to rendezvous at the points indicated, also to kill and destroy as enemies of the country wherever they may be found, all such hostile Indians.
>
> And further, as the only reward I am authorized to offer for such services, I hereby empower such citizens, or parties of citizens, to take captive, and hold to their private use and benefit, all the property of said hostile Indians, that they may capture.

Among those who responded to Governor Evans' call was Colonel John M. Chivington. This man was highly respected. He had been a Methodist preacher, an abolitionist, and the commander of the Colorado Volunteer Troops who had destroyed a Confederate supply train in a battle in New Mexico. Now he took command of the Third Colorado Cavalry. He marched these men to a point near Fort Lyons, where Cheyenne under Black Kettle and White Antelope, and Arapaho under Left Hand, had camped.

The Sand Creek Massacre

These Indians had thought they were doing as the governor had requested. They were camped on Sand Creek as the Commanding Officer at Fort Lyons had asked. They were not leaving the camp except to pick up rations at the fort or to hunt. They were completely surprised, when at dawn on November 29, 1864, they were attacked. George Bent was in the camp that day. He was later to write:

> At dawn . . . I was still in bed when I heard shouts and the noise of people running about the camp. I jumped up and ran out of my lodge. From down the creek a large body of troops was advancing at a rapid trot, some to the east of the camps, and others on the opposite side of the creek, to the west. More soldiers could be seen making for the Indian

George Bent, from an engraving made sometime after Sand Creek.
—SHSC

pony herds to the south of the camps; in the camps themselves all was confusion and noise—men, women, and children rushing out of the lodges partly dressed; women and children screaming at the sight of the troops; men running back into the lodges for their arms, other men, already armed, or with lassos and bridles in their hands, running for the herds to attempt to get some of the ponies before the troops could reach the animals and drive them off.

I looked toward the chief's lodge and saw that Black Kettle had a large American flag tied to the end of a long lodgepole and was standing in front of his lodge, holding the pole, with the flag fluttering in the grey light of the winter dawn. I heard him call to the people not to be afraid, that the soldiers would not hurt them; then the troops opened fire from two sides of the camps.

The Indians all began running, but they did not seem to know what to do or where to turn. The women and children were screaming and wailing . . . . We ran up the creek with the cavalry following us, one company on each bank, keeping right after us and firing all the time. Many of the people had preceeded us up the creek, and the dry bed of the stream was now a terrible sight: men, women, and children lying thickly scattered on the sand, some dead and the rest too badly wounded to move . . . . Here the troops kept us besieged until darkness came on.

An artist's idea of what took place at Sand Creek.
—SHSC

That night, Colonel Chivington wrote a letter to his commanding officer:

Headquarters District of
Colorado in the Field,
On Big Bend of Sandy Creek,
Colorado Territory
November 29, 1864

Charles Wheeler
A.A.A. General
Headquarters District of Colorado
Denver, Colorado

Sir:

I have not the time to give you a detailed history of our engagement of to-day or to mention those officers and men who distinguished themselves in one of the most bloody Indian battles ever fought on these plains. You will find enclosed the report of my surgeon in charge, which will bring to many anxious friends the sad fate of loved ones, who are and have been risking everything to avenge the horrid deeds of those savages we have so severely handled. We made a forced march of forty miles and surprised, at break of day, one of the most powerful villages of the Cheyenne nation, and captured over five hundred animals; killing the celebrated chiefs One Eye, White Antelope, Knock-Knee, Black Kettle, and Little Robe, with about five hundred of their people, destroying all their lodges and equipage, making almost an annihilation of the entire tribe.

I shall leave here, as soon as I can see our wounded safely on the way to the hospital at Fort Lyon, for the villages of the Sioux, which are reported about eighty miles from here on the Smoky Hill, and three thousand strong—so look out for more fighting. I will state for the consideration of gentlemen who are opposed to fighting these red scoundrels, that I was shown by my chief surgeon the scalp of a white man, taken from the lodge of one of the chiefs, which could not have been more than two or three days taken: and I could mention many more things to show how these Indians, who have been drawing government rations at Fort Lyon, are and have been acting.

Very respectfully, your obedient servant,
J.M. Chivington
Colonel, Commanding Colorado Expedition
against Indians on Plains

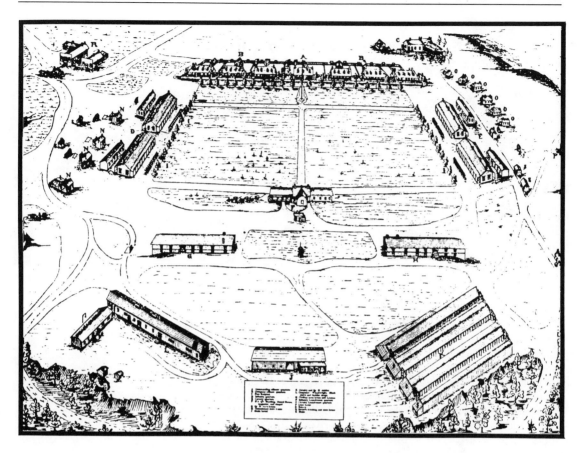

Fort Lyon as it appeared when Chivington led his cavalry against the Indians camped at Sand Creek.

Chivington's report was not quite accurate; Black Kettle was not killed that day. He was not to die until four years later when George Custer's troops attacked a village along the Washita River. He was right about White Antelope, however. A Cheyenne leader, White Antelope knew that Sand Creek was the end of the tribe's traditional culture. When he realized that the troops were gunning down his fellow Indians, he decided it was the day for him to die. He stood still in front of his lodge and sang his death song:

Nothing lives long,
Only the earth and the mountains.

For a while after the Sand Creek Massacre, the Indians retaliated by attacking settlers on the Colorado High Plains. Julesburg, a stage station on the Platte in the northeast, was repeatedly burned; there was a desperate battle at Beecher's

Island; and, finally, the last battle with the Plains Indians in Colorado Territory took place at Summit Springs near what is now Sterling, Colorado.

Colorado's Last Indian War

One hundred Pawnee scouts under Captain Luther H. North and his brother, Captain Frank North, with William F. "Buffalo Bill" Cody as their guide, set out with eight companies of the Fifth Cavalry. They meant to find and destroy the power of a large group of Cheyenne, Sioux, and Arapaho who had been attacking and looting settlements in Nebraska and Kansas. They were successful at Summit Springs. Frank North described the event in his diary:

> Sunday, July 11, 1869. Marched this morn at 6 A.M. with fifty of my men and two hundred whites, with three days' rations. Follow trail until three P.M. and came up to the village. Made a grand charge and it was a complete victory. Took the whole village of about 85 lodges. Killed about sixty Indians. Took about seventeen prisoners and about three hundred ponies and robes, etc., innumerable. Rained pretty hard tonight.

The Ute Indians were able to hold onto their land a bit longer. Eventually, however, they too were to find themselves in the way of white settlement. When settlers moved onto the Western Slope, the Utes began their series of losing battles.

*Plains Indians after their
removal to a reservation.
—National Archives*

These drawings were found at the site of the Summit Springs battle. They are a part of a sketchbook filled with such drawings.

QUESTIONS:

1. Why might the Arapahos have felt comfortable with whites during the Gold Rush days? How did this change? Why did it change?

2. Why did Greeley and William Bent think that the Indians ought to become farmers? Would the history of these native Americans have been different if the Civil War had not occurred when it did?

3. Why did the citizens of Denver feel that the Sand Creek Massacre was justified?

4. How did the Indians feel? What did they do after the battle?

5. Why were the Utes able to hold onto their land a little longer?

ACTIVITIES:

1. Draw a series of pictures of one of the Indian battles as the Indians themselves might have drawn it.

2. Pretend that the Indian wars had turned out differently and the settlers were the ones to have been placed on reservations. Write a report in which you describe how you as a settler felt about that, and how you went about organizing your life on the reservation.

3. Find out which of the Indian battles took place near your home. Research the battle and explain the event to the class.

4. Read one of the books about the Indian wars in Colorado and report on the events. You might want to do this with a classmate with each of you reporting from the point of view of the two different groups involved—the white Americans and the native Americans.

Books you might enjoy:

Dee Brown. *Action at Beecher Island*. New York: Curtis Books, 1967. Based on diaries, letters, and other firsthand accounts, this is the story of the nine-day siege of U.S. Army Scouts by Plains Indians in 1868. Parts of the book are written as fiction, but it is probably quite accurate.

David C. Cooke. *Indians on the Warpath*. New York: Dodd, Meade & Co., 1951. Provides a good account of the last of the Indian Wars, some of which took place in Colorado.

Edith Dorian and W.N. Wilson. *Hoka Hey, American Indians Then and Now*. New York: Whittlesey House, McGraw Hill, 1957. This book describes the changes that have occurred in Indian life from the time of first white contact until fairly recent times.

Howard M. Fast. *The Last Frontier*. New York: Duell, Loan, and Pearce, 1941. An exciting fictional account of the end of the traditional way of life of the Plains Indians.

Richard Wiengardt. *Sound the Charge: Spillman Creek to Summit Springs*. Englewood, Co: Jacqueline Enterprises, 1978. An account of the major battles, skirmishes, and raids that took place in Colorado during white settlement.

Unit II

Unit II

Colorado		United States	
1859	Pike's Peak Rush	1859	First producing oil well
1860	Population 34,277	1860	Population 31,443,321
1861	Named & becomes territory	1861–65	Civil War
1868	Hill's smelter opens	1869	Transcontinental railroad completed
1870	Railroad reaches Denver	1873	Economic crash and depression
1876	Statehood	1876	Centennial
1878	Leadville boom	1877	Telephone patented
1880	Population 194, 327	1880	Population 50,155,783
1881–82	Ute removal; Western Slope opened to settlement	1884	*Adventures of Huckleberry Finn* published
1885–86	Cattle frontier ends	1889	First electric automobile
1891	Cripple Creek Rush	1893	Chicago World's Fair and economic crash
1899	First car in Denver	1896	Election McKinley vs. Bryan
1900	Population 539,700	1900	Population 75,994,575

—7—
Miners

"PIKE'S PEAK—GOLD EXCITEMENT IN THE CITY
—A NEW CALIFORNIA."
This headline greeted the reader of the *Leavenworth Times* (Kansas), September 11, 1858. In Kansas and elsewhere the news of a new gold discovery was in the wind.

Gold! The thought of it excited many people beyond reason and drove them to go and get it. The attraction, of course, was to get richer than anyone had ever dreamed, without having to work a lifetime. Unfortunately, most men and women who rushed to Colorado to find their pot of gold did not get rich. What they found was hard work under very difficult conditions. The rewards usually fell far short of the dreams. As one person said, "I never worked so hard in my life, to get rich without working."

Legends and Rumors

The very first Europeans who traveled to what became Colorado were looking for gold or silver. The Spanish from New Mexico searched for minerals in this land to the north. They left behind names for places they had been (Animas River), minerals they sought (La Plata Mountains, meaning silver), and legends of lost mines. They did not stay very long and did not find great wealth.

When explorer Zebulon Pike was in Santa Fe in 1807, he heard interesting news from mountain man James Purcell. Purcell told Pike that he had found gold at the place where the Platte River begins. In the following years other stories about gold in the mountains began to reach the American settlements back in Missouri. One story even claimed that gold bullets were being shot by Indians in their guns.

Meanwhile, Spain lost most of what is today Colorado, to Mexico. Then Mexico lost Colorado to the United States in 1848 at the end of the Mexican War. Hardly a year later the California gold rush started. Gold seekers went north and south of Colorado to get to California, since Colorado's mountains were too high for them to travel over. Some of these forty-niners, as they were called, did stop for a little while, however, to look for gold along the foothills of Colorado's Rocky Mountains.

A party of Cherokee Indians from what is now Oklahoma passed by the future site of Denver in June 1850. One of them wrote in his diary on June 22, "gold found." It was discovered in Ralston Creek on the future site of Arvada. There was not enough gold to tempt them to stay, and they went on to California. The Cherokees did not have much luck there, and they eventually returned home. But they could not forget about the gold they had found along the Rockies on their trip. In the winter of 1857–58 some of them decided to go back and search again.

The Cherokees did not know that another group of men from the town of Lawrence, Kansas had the same idea. They were interested in the Rocky Mountains because of a story they had heard from a Delaware Indian, Fall Leaf. He had gone west with the army as a scout and brought back some gold. Of course, his neighbors were very interested in it and made plans to find the place where it had been found.

That spring both groups started west. William Green Russell, who had mined in Georgia and California, led the men from Oklahoma, including the Cherokees. They were the first to arrive. After weeks of disappointment, they finally found several hundred dollars' worth of gold at the place that is now Denver. The Lawrence party heard about the Russell party's success and hurried to join it. So did a trader by the name of John Cantrell, who was on his way back east. Cantrell took a small amount of gold with him and became the Paul Revere of the Colorado gold rush. He told everyone he met about the discovery.

Because of Cantrell's story about the gold, a newspaper in Kansas City used this headline on August 26, 1858: "The New Eldorado!!! Gold in Kansas Territory." (Much of eastern Colorado was then part of Kansas.) More reports of gold came back and Americans grew excited. Many wanted to go to the Pike's Peak country, as it was called then. They were sure that fortune awaited them, if they could only get there first.

Pike's Peak Gold Rush

That winter of 1858–59 was exciting. Many, many people planned to go west as soon as they could. They were afraid that if they waited too long all the gold would be gone. They made plans, talked endlessly of gold, purchased a wagon and horses, mules, or oxen to pull it, equipment, food, and a guidebook to tell them how to get there. Then they dreamed about how much gold they would find. They could hardly wait.

Spring finally came. It was like the firing of a gun to start a race—somewhere around 100,000 fifty-niners rushed west. Most of them rode in wagons or on horseback. A few walked and some pushed handcarts all the way. One group purchased tickets to ride a wind wagon. Its owner promised that his wagon with a sail would get them there faster and more comfortably than anything else could. Unfortunately for him and his passengers, the wagon "sank" by running into a gully. Their dreams ended right there on the prairie.

Meanwhile, out in the Pike's Peak country, not much gold was being mined. A few hardy souls actually arrived before the winter snows closed the overland trails. They organized towns that became Boulder and Denver and waited for the snow in the mountains to melt so they could go into the hills to prospect, although a few brave men did go into the mountains west of Denver and Boulder that winter.

In January 1859, George Jackson discovered gold near the future town of Idaho Springs. The bitter cold, snow, and frozen ground drove him out. That same month a group of men found gold above Boulder at a place they called Gold Hill. Finally, in April, John Gregory, another experienced miner, made the biggest discovery yet, between soon-to-be Central City and Black Hawk. All these men tried to keep their finds a secret. They wanted to be the first to mine as soon as spring returned to the mountains.

While these things were going on in the mountains, the fifty-niners began arriving in Denver. They soon learned that very little gold had been found there. Denver was only a collection of log cabins and it was very expensive to live there. Few people wanted to venture into the mountains until the weather was better. Disappointed by what they found, many turned around and went home. Others on their way west heard of the troubles and turned around before they even reached Colorado. Newspapers, which had been praising the region only a few months before, now called it a failure, a "humbug."

It was fortunate for Colorado that the ones who had discovered gold could not keep it a secret. By May the news was out, and now people rushed into the mountains with their picks and pans. About 25,000 of the nearly 100,000 fifty-niners who started west had stayed; the rest had given up and left.

Gold Mining

When they came to the site of the gold diggings, these would-be miners found the work hard, tiring, and long. Most of them had never mined before in their lives. They had to learn by watching the experienced miners or by trial and error. It looked easy enough; all you needed was a pick, a shovel, a pan, and a strong back. When you found a spot that looked good, you staked your claim to let everyone else know that it was yours. Then the diggings could be worked. Gravel was placed in a pan, where it was washed. By swirling water around the pan and gently washing the gravel, the lighter materials would float away. The gold, which is a very heavy mineral, would stay in the pan. If you were lucky, there would be some gold left at the bottom. The process seemed simple, but it took a lot of skill and hard work. Because some of the fifty-niners were experienced miners, they soon built rockers and sluice boxes, which let them wash much more gold-bearing gravel in less time. This was called placer mining, or the mining of free gold, which is gold found on the surface or in stream beds. Hard rock mining involves digging deeply into the earth and mining gold ore from a vein. Placer mining predominated in Colorado during 1859.

The 1859 gold rush had happened so quickly that there was not time to organize local governments or courts. This did not bother the miners at all—they quickly formed their own mining districts, miners' laws, and miners' courts. This gave them a way to file and record their claims. They also had a court to settle any arguments. For example, if someone "jumped" your claim (tried to take it from you and say it was his), you could take your case to a jury of your neighbors to decide who was right.

Everywhere gold was found mining districts and little mining camps grew almost overnight—Georgetown, Fairplay, Breckenridge, Oro City, and Nevadaville, to mention a few. Miners did not have the time to raise crops or make their own clothes. They wanted only to mine and make money. But they did have the money to buy goods and entertainment. So other people came—storekeepers, blacksmiths, saloonkeepers, bootmakers, carpenters—to serve their needs. Soon these were

Miners are using a sluice box. The gravel washed down the long trough, where the gold, heavier than other metals and rock, sank to the bottom and was trapped behind wooden riffles, or bars. Sometimes miners used a rocker, which looked like a baby's cradle.
—U.S. Geological Survey

joined by lawyers, doctors, school teachers (because families soon arrived, too), and ministers, and a community was organized.

Denver became the largest town. Although little gold was ever found there, it was most newcomers' destination. The stagecoaches also traveled to Denver, once they established regular service. Freighters brought their wagonfuls of food, equipment, and other supplies there. It was then shipped to the mountain districts. Denver was a storage and a shipping point, the gateway to the mountains. Denver also hoped to become the capital of the new territory that was being created by this rush of people.

Government is Organized

Almost immediately, the fifty-niners realized that there had to be some legal basis for their settlement. Eastern Colorado was divided between Kansas and Nebraska territories, both of which were too far east to govern the newly settled area very well. These pioneers had created mining districts, and now they thought they could create their own territory. They called it Jefferson Territory and asked the United States Congress to approve their action. Congress refused, because it was determined to create the territory and establish the government under federal rules.

Unfortunately, Congress was having a difficult time in 1860–61 because of the problem of slavery. Northerners and Southerners were angry and divided over this question. The South wanted slave owning to be allowed; the North thought it should be abolished and the slaves freed. This was one of the disputes that led to the Civil War. Congress could hardly talk about anything without slavery being brought up. The future of the Pike's Peak mines depended on the outcome of the slavery issue because the South feared this would be a free territory. After some southern states left the United States to form their own government, the remaining northern congressmen finally organized a new territory and called it Colorado. The date of its birth was February 28, 1861.

President Abraham Lincoln selected the first governor for Colorado Territory. He chose a man who had long been interested in the West, William Gilpin, who arrived in Denver in May, 1861.

Colorado was now a United States territory. This meant that the governor, judges, and other officers would be appointed by the President. The local voters could elect their own legislators and a territorial delegate to represent Colorado in Washington. Whenever Colorado had enough settlers, it could apply for statehood, and, if accepted, it would become an equal partner in the union with the other states. This would take time, but it was something that many Coloradans wanted right from the start.

By the summer of 1861, Colorado was named, had a territorial government, and had developed an economy based upon mining. It had come a long way since those exciting days of the spring of 1859. But there were troubles as well as blessings.

Wells Fargo was a famous stagecoach company that carried passengers, mail, and bullion to and from Colorado. This is its Denver office in the late 1860s.
—First National Bank

Hard Rock Mining

The main problem was in mining. The placer diggings were neither as rich nor as large as everyone had thought. The amounts of gold being found soon decreased, but the miners did not give up. Instead they began to dig into the mountainsides to look for more gold, using a new form of mining called hard rock, deep, or quartz mining.

The gold they were looking for was locked in a vein. They had to pick and blast it out of this vein; it was rough, dangerous work. But that was just the beginning. The ore had to be taken to the surface and then crushed to separate the gold from other minerals. This involves greater skills, more equipment, a knowledge of many more aspects of mining, and is much more costly than placer mining. Most of Colorado's mining has been of the hard rock kind.

As soon as the miners began digging into the mountains, they had problems. Water flooded some of the mines, and pumps had to be installed to get rid of it. The underground workings needed to be timbered, using logs and wood beams, to keep the earth from collapsing onto the miners. To get the ore to the surface, eventually a hoist, or cage (like an elevator), was devised. Skilled miners were needed. The fifty-niner miners usually did not have the experience or the money to do this type of mining.

The biggest problem of all was finding a way to separate the gold from the rock when it got to the surface. It was easy enough to crush the ore in a stamp mill, but the problem was what to do next. Many methods were tried, but the gold was not being separated and saved. Sometimes more than half of it was lost with the waste materials that went out on the tailings pile. The miners and millmen did not know what to do to solve the problem, and by the mid-1860s, Colorado mining was in serious trouble. People began to leave Colorado.

At this point a young chemistry professor, Nathaniel Hill, arrived on the scene. He had traveled to Colorado in 1864 to check on some mining property. Fascinated by the milling problems, he became determined to solve them. Hill knew that a fortune awaited the person who could find the answer to separating out the gold. For three years he studied and experimented, even traveling to England to see how smelters there worked ore. Finally he developed a process, and in 1868 he opened a smelter in Black Hawk, near Central City. His solution worked, and Colorado mining made a comeback. Hill's smelter became the best known one in the territory.

Something else happened, too. In 1870 the railroad came

to Denver, allowing both cheaper and faster transportation. Now, instead of weeks or even months, people and freight could arrive in Denver in days. This helped mining tremendously. Within ten years railroads had reached Central City, Georgetown, and Boulder, and plans were being made to lay tracks elsewhere.

Silver

One other factor put Colorado mining on the road to recovery. Silver was discovered, and Colorado then had two rich minerals to mine. Silver had been found near Georgetown in 1864 and across the mountains in Summit County in 1865. Unfortunately, silver proved to be even harder to separate than gold. So again the miners had to wait for a smelting process. Lorenzo Bowman, a black man from Missouri, came up with a method that helped somewhat, but it did not provide the final answer. However, thanks to Hill and others, silver smelting developed rapidly, and by the 1870s Colorado smelters could handle many of the silver-bearing ores.

The successful silver-smelting process came just in time. Just as the 1860s had been the golden sixties, silver was queen of the seventies and for twenty years afterward. In the 1870s silver was found all the way from Boulder County in the north to Dolores County in the southwest. Before these ten years were over, it seemed as though silver was being found under nearly every rock or on every mountain. Colorado, by the end of the 1870s, became the United States' greatest mining state. The dreams of 1859 had come true, not with gold, but with silver. And the pattern was the same: first the discoveries, excitement, rushes, organization of mining districts, the start of mining camps, and then the settling down to actual mining. One mining rush quickly followed another.

Caribou, in Boulder County, was the first of the 1870s silver booms. It was being found there in 1869 and the rush came in 1870. The camp went through ups and downs for a decade before the rich silver played out. Caribou's days of glory ended, and it soon became a ghost town. This was the fate of most Colorado mining communities.

One exception to this fate was Georgetown. It came to be Colorado's first "silver queen," the district with the richest mines and the greatest population. Because it had richer mines

than Caribou, Georgetown attracted more publicity, invest-
ments, and eventually a railroad. Silver and gold were mined
there for many years, and Georgetown became one of the
state's major mining towns. It had churches, schools, railroad
connections, a large business district, and smelters. Unlike
many now-dead silver towns, Georgetown has survived.

Leadville

Nothing in Colorado mining was more thrilling than the
Leadville silver discoveries of 1877–78. Both Georgetown and
Central City seemed dull in comparison. Not since 1858–59
had so much mining fever swept Colorado.

Mary Hallock Foote, a writer and artist, went there in 1879
at the height of the rush. She wrote a friend, "All Roads Lead
to Leadville. Everybody was going there! Our fellow citizens
as we saw them from the road were more picturesque than
pleasing. I was absorbed by this curious exhibition of humanity
all along the 70 mile long journey." Leadville fascinated Mrs.
Foote, and it also fascinated Americans throughout the country. Newspaper reporters and journalists flocked to Leadville
to write about "the Magic City."

Leadville had not always attracted so much attention. Prospectors had come to the area in 1860 and found some rich
placer diggings at what they called California Gulch. Within
a few years these gold diggings were mined out, and the people
drifted away. In the following years, the few who stayed continued to mine, but nobody thought much of the region. Why
should anyone go there when richer districts beckoned? In the
end, those who stayed were rewarded. Suddenly, in 1877, rich
silver deposits were found and Leadville was born. By 1880
the census takers counted nearly 15,000 people there, although
some claimed the number went as high as 20,000. In either
case, Leadville ranked second only to Denver in population.
Not bad for a city only three years old.

Just as Leadville gained instant fame and made Colorado a
familiar name both here and abroad, its miners astonished the
mining world. In 1879 over $9 million worth of silver was
mined; the next year the total topped $11 million. When the
figures for lead and gold were added to these, it was easy to
see that Leadville was a mineral treasure box. Colorado had
never seen anything like it before.

Leadville produced legends. None is better known today than that of Horace Tabor. Tabor had been a fifty-niner miner, without much success. He had mined at Idaho Springs and then, in 1860, had come to California Gulch, where he opened a store, while also mining. With the help of his hardworking wife, Augusta, Tabor managed to make a decent living. The Tabors moved across the mountains to Buckskin Joe and then back to Oro City at the head of California Gulch. The mining riches Tabor sought still eluded him. He continually grub-staked prospectors; that is, he gave them food and supplies from his store in return for a share of any mines they found. It appeared that Tabor was going to spend his life on the fringe of Colorado mining without ever being rich or famous.

Suddenly everything changed in 1877, when he moved to Leadville. Although he was the second merchant in the community, Tabor hoped that maybe now his opportunity for fortune had come. And so it had. Tabor grubstaked two prospectors, who found the Little Pittsburg Mine. Other rich mine discoveries soon followed and very quickly Augusta and Horace were millionaires. Tabor came to symbolize the story of Leadville and Colorado mining. After twenty years he had succeeded. This was what all fifty-niners had hoped to do—the Tabors were among the lucky few.

The Silver State

Until well into the 1890s, prospectors and miners searched for silver ore with hardly a pause. And they found it. They found it in the Gunnison country and in the San Juans. They found it at Silver Cliff in the Wet Mountain Valley and in other places. Many communities followed Caribou's path, quickly becoming ghost towns; a few lasted and became permanent.

Only one camp and district rivaled Leadville for any period of time. That was Aspen. Silver gave Aspen its start, not skiing, for which it is world famous today. Aspen soon had railroads and smelters and, by the 1890s, it had almost passed Leadville as the number one silver mining district. By then Colorado was mining over $20,000,000 worth of silver per year and began calling itself the Silver State. Nothing seemed to threaten its prosperity or its future.

There was a very dark cloud growing on the horizon, how-

Augusta Tabor was a fifty-niner. She and her husband Horace lived in several mining communities before they hit a silver bonanza at Leadville. Augusta ran their store, served as postmaster, helped carry gold to Denver, cooked for miners and nursed them when they were sick.
—Colorado Historical Society

ever. The price of silver was falling. A number of things caused this to happen. Many countries stopped making silver coins. Only a few industrial uses for silver had been developed, so there were not many people who wanted to buy it. Jewelry could not use large amounts of the metal. Finally, so much silver was being mined that there was just too much of it on the market. That made the price of it fall from $1.32 an ounce in 1870 to $.87 in 1892. Miners worried about this, hoping the problem would somehow be solved and the price would go up again.

In 1893 Colorado and the whole United States suddenly plunged into a severe economic depression. When that happened, banks failed, businesses closed, and people lost their jobs. All these things occurred at once. Mining was hurt by what was happening, especially when the price of silver dropped another $.20 per ounce. It was no longer profitable to mine silver, so the mines closed, throwing miners out of work. The silver mining communities were badly hurt; their whole future depended on silver. All of Colorado suffered, because silver had been the backbone of the state's economy.

Colorado had never seen anything like this before. It seemed to Coloradans that they suffered more than anyone else in the country. Perhaps they did; times were very bad. Colorado's people wondered if the state would ever regain the prosperity it had known for the past twenty years. Fortunately, it was saved again by its mineral treasures.

Cripple Creek

Back in 1859 Pike's Peak was the best-known geographic point in the central Rockies. Although it gave its name to the gold rush, no gold had been found there. In the 1890s, however, the story changed. Southwest of Pike's Peak, a place called Cripple Creek would become Colorado's greatest gold district.

A wandering cowboy by the name of Bob Womack gets the credit for the discovery. He found gold ore there in the 1880s, but had a terrible time convincing others. Finally he did, and in the early 1890s the rush started. It came just in time to take some of the sting out of the collapse of silver and the 1890s depression. Many little camps were established, but the district was dominated by two communities, Cripple Creek and Victor. No mining towns were more famous in their day than these two.

Mining camps could boom and die in a season or two. The lucky ones grew and prospered. These two photographs show Colorado's famous gold mining town of Cripple Creek in 1892 (opposite, above) and 1893 (opposite, below). It is July 4, 1893, and the town and people are celebrating.
—Colorado Historical Society

The Cripple Creek district produced many millionaires, but the most famous was Winfield Scott Stratton. Like Tabor, Stratton had spent a long time on the Colorado mining frontier without great success. He had gone to Leadville and elsewhere and had studied techniques, but to no avail. When he went to Cripple Creek, however, Stratton finally was handsomely rewarded for his time. His Independence Mine, which he discovered on July 4, 1891, made him a millionaire several times over. He later sold it for $10 million, and there was no income tax in those days.

Cripple Creek was the last of the great nineteenth-century Colorado mining rushes. By now the days of the prospector were far behind. Mining had become big business. The mines were owned by large companies or stockholders who often lived somewhere else. The chances for making big money at Cripple Creek were high, but so were the costs of mining.

Most of the men at Cripple Creek never owned a mine. They were miners who simply worked for someone else for a day's pay. Because of the low pay and the lack of opportunity for better jobs, the miners joined labor unions. In 1894 a strike broke out over low wages and long working hours. The miners won this struggle and gained an eight-hour day at $3-a-day wages. They were obviously happy with the results, but some of the owners and companies were not. The strike left a lot of bitterness.

Colorado mining had come a long way since 1859—from the day of the lonely miner with his pick and pan to that of the large company and the hired miner. Colorado had been fortunate that it had both gold and silver and other metals and fuels. Many western mining states had not been so lucky, and their mining days were over. But for Colorado, it was the single most important factor in the economy during the last forty years of the nineteenth century. It created jobs, encouraged railroad building, made the state famous, and helped bring in investment money. Farms, ranches, business, and manufacturing all benefited. Camps and towns were established and grew because of mining. Most of Colorado's political leaders had ties to mining or mining backgrounds. In the years that followed the Pike's Peak rush, mining had done what people had expected it to do back in 1859. Without it, Colorado's growth and development would have been much slower and much different. Mining and miners became a legend in their own day—and our own.

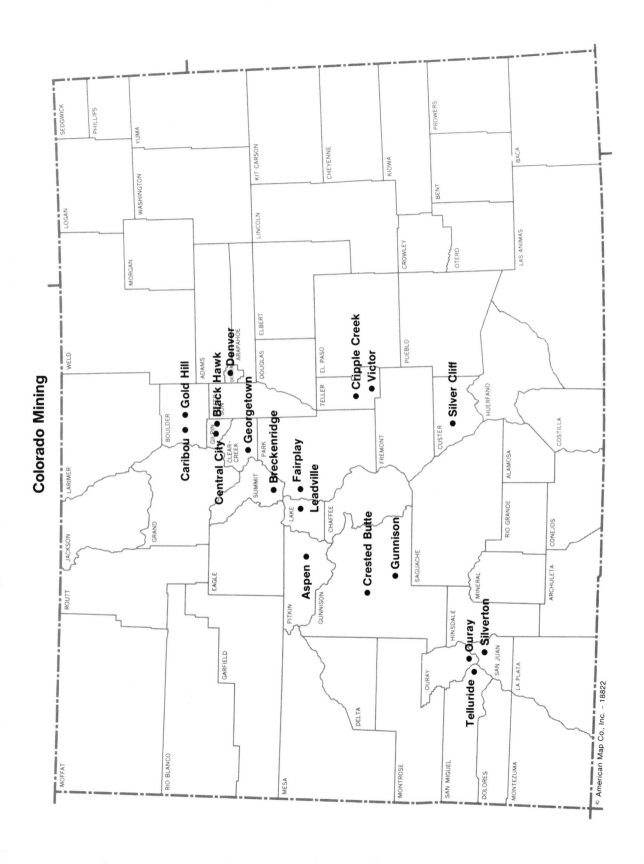

Colorado Mining

© American Map Co., Inc. – 18822

DID YOU KNOW:

- That in 1899 miners were paid the following wages:

Hardrock miners (9 hrs.)	$3.00
Machine drill men (9 hrs.)	$4.00
Laborers, surface (10 hrs.)	$2.00–2.50
Coal miners (per ton mined)	60¢
Mule drivers (per day)	$2.50–3.00

QUESTIONS:

1. Examine the map on p. 117 and then explain why the Spanish, when they found little mineral wealth in their explorations of Colorado, lost interest in the area.

2. Why is John Cantrell known as the "Paul Revere of the Gold Rush"?

3. What means of transportation did the fifty-niners use?

4. What did it mean to "stake a claim"? What happened if someone "jumped" your claim?

5. What started the gold rush of 1860? How successful was it?

6. How did the problem of slavery affect the establishment of Colorado Territory?

7. What is the difference between placer and hard rock mining?

8. Describe some of the problems of hard rock mining.

9. Why is Nathaniel Hill considered a Colorado hero?

10. Compare the impact of gold mining to silver mining on the state of Colorado.

Books you might enjoy:

Anne Ellis. *Life of an Ordinary Woman.* Lincoln: University of Nebraska Press, 1980 (reprint). Colorado from the view of the miner's family.

Mabel B. Lee. *Cripple Creek Days.* New York: Doubleday, 1958. Cripple Creek as remembered by a young girl. Fascinating.

Duane A. Smith. *Colorado Mining: A Photographic History.* Albuquerque: University of New Mexico Press, 1977.

Muriel S. Wolle. *Stampede to Timberline.* Chicago: Sage Books, 1974. History and human interest. Read it—you'll have fun.

—8—
Townspeople

The mining frontier was an urban frontier; that is, camps and towns were built at the same time the miners came. This was different from the cattle and farming frontiers, where towns usually came quite some time after the first settlers. Miners and townspeople arrived nearly together. The miners did not have time to raise crops, manufacture their equipment, or haul in their supplies. But they did have gold and silver to pay others to do those things for them. Therefore, people came and settled in communities along the foothills and in the mining districts.

Denver

Of all the communities, Denver quickly stood out as the most important. Although it was not near the mines, it had a good location, close to two of the gateways to the mountains, Clear Creek Canyon and the South Platte River. It also had the advantage of being well known to the miners, since it was the point to which fifty-niners first traveled. There had once been several settlements in the area, but Denver won out over them all.

From 1859 to the present Denver has been the center of Colorado's trade and commerce. It seems that this grocer sold almost every kind of food.
—Colorado Historical Society

Of Denver's early rivals, Golden proved hardest to overcome. Golden was closer to the mountains and Clear Creek Canyon. Both these towns wanted to be the capital of the territory. They served alternately as capital until Denver finally gained the honor permanently. It was not until 1881, however, that Denver officially became the state capital. Although Denver beat Golden on this issue, the two remained business rivals for years.

Even with its advantages, Denver had problems during its early years. In April 1863 fire burned out the center of the city—seventy buildings were destroyed. Fire was always greatly feared in these communities where wood was the main construction material. Denver rebuilt with brick and bounced back, before a second disaster came on May 20, 1864. Cherry Creek flooded, washing away the *Rocky Mountain News* office and other buildings and killing eleven people. The town had been built along the banks of the creek and the South Platte River. Some longtime residents and Indians had warned the settlers about flash floods, but they were in too much of a hurry to build a town to listen to the warnings.

Nothing could stop Denver's townbuilders. The fire and flood damage was quickly repaired and life went on as before. Then came more bad news. Mining, on which Denver's future depended, declined, hurting Denver's businesses. The Indian troubles of 1863–65 slowed growth even more. By far the worst news, however, was that plans for the transcontinental railroad showed that it would bypass Denver. It would go north through Julesburg and on to Cheyenne, Wyoming, instead of coming to Denver. This was very serious indeed. During these years the town without a railroad had very little chance of growing. The railroad was the cheapest, fastest, most comfortable, and the only dependable, year-round means of transportation. A community just had to have railroad connections.

Denver's leaders tried to change the plans of the Union Pacific Railroad, but failed to do so. They decided the only thing to do was to build their own railroad, if they wanted to keep Denver from becoming nearly a ghost town. To make matters worse, some of Golden's businessmen decided to do the same thing, and the race was on.

It took courage for either town to start such a project. Railroad building was costly, and money was scarce in Colorado.

But Denver's business people and leaders worked hard and with lots of will power. They built the Denver Pacific, to connect Denver with the Union Pacific line at Cheyenne. In 1870, a silver spike, a gift from Georgetown, was driven to celebrate the completion of Denver's railroad. Golden had lost again and would not seriously challenge its rival after this.

Denver had been very lucky. Its ambitious leaders had looked into the future and planned well, overcoming many setbacks in the process. Several other railroads soon reached the town, and it became a major business and trading center. Before long Denver had the best theaters, schools, and hospitals in Colorado and the richest banks. Industry also began on a small scale. In 1878 Nathaniel Hill moved his smelter from Black Hawk to make Denver a smelting center. He came to Denver because of its transportation advantages, to be near the coal fields, and because of the lower cost of living.

Hill was not the only one who moved to the city. Others were attracted for similar reasons. Denver grew from 4,700 to 106,000 people between 1860 and 1890; it was Colorado's largest city.

Its success caused jealousy in other communities that wanted to be as big and important as Denver. None of them was able to match the "Queen City," though. For a short time Central City thought it was the best, but when gold mining declined, so did Central, as it was then called. Leadville challenged Denver briefly too, at the same time that much of its silver wealth was going to help build Denver. For example, Horace Tabor built a lavish grand opera house in Denver that cost $850,000. There was none finer between Kansas City and San Francisco. Cripple Creek had gold and sudden growth, but by then it was no contest. Denver reigned supreme.

Other Communities

The mountain mining communities and the settlements along the foothills were the start of Colorado's urbanization— the growth of its cities and towns. They not only provided the core of permanent settlement, they also helped develop the economy and plans for the future. These towns were in some ways similar to the ones you know today, but in other ways they were quite different.

In appearance they were certainly different. A visitor from

England, Isabella Bird, was not impressed by Longmont. She described it this way:

> . . . a wide straggling street, in which glaring frame houses and a few shops stand opposite to each other. A two-story house, one of the whitest and most glaring, and without a veranda like all the others, is the "St. Vrain Hotel," called after the St. Vrain River, out of which the ditch is taken which enables Longmont to exist.

She did not care for Boulder either:

> Boulder is a hideous collection of frame houses on a burning plain, but it aspires to be a "city" in virtue of being a "distributing point" for the settlements up the Boulder Canyon, and of the discovery of a coal seam.

Writer Sara Jane Lippincott visited Black Hawk in September 1871 and described what she saw:

> Narrow and dingy as is this mining town, its people are making a brave effort to give it a look of comfort, in pleasant private dwellings, neat churches and fine school-buildings, perched up against the mountain-side, where it would seem no building larger than a miner's hut could find lodgement. Scarcely a tree or shrub is to be seen, or even a flower, except it be in some parlor window . . . .

When you lived in the mountains, growing a garden or a lawn successfully was a real accomplishment. Many people wondered why they should go to the trouble when they would soon be moving on to some new mining district anyway. For the same reason not many people worried about painting their homes.

You might wonder why people moved frequently. A teenager by the name of Irving Howbert lived in Hamilton (in South Park) in the summer of 1860. He commented that "two or three times that summer, there was what was known as a 'stampede' from Hamilton to reported new discoveries." What started it? "These stampedes usually originated from a prospector coming to town and telling a friend, as a great secret, of rich placers he had discovered." As soon as they heard about a new discovery, people hurried off expecting to find a fortune.

Living in town meant that you had more of the "modern" conveniences and other advantages than your friends out in the rural areas. Here were found a greater variety of stores. In May 1878, for instance, Leadville had 2 each of drugstores, banks, restaurants, dry goods stores, and bakeries, 3 meat markets, livery stables, and barber shops, and 4 general stores. In the spring of 1879 the city had such amazing totals as 20 meat markets, 31 restaurants, 51 groceries, 17 barber shops, and 4 banks. Leadville, of course, was booming then because of its silver, but other towns also had the same kinds of businesses in smaller numbers.

At first the cost of living in all these communities was very high. Horace Greeley visited Denver in 1859 and was shocked at the high prices. He wrote in his newspaper column:

> To the bread, bacon, and beans, which formed the staple of every meal a short time ago, there have been several recent additions; milk, which was last week twenty-five cents per quart, is now down to ten, and I hear a rumor that eggs, owing to a recent increase in the number of hens, within five hundred miles, from four or five to twelve or fifteen, are about to fall from a dollar a dozen to fifty cents per dozen.

The cities depended on the farmer for food. Here farm wagons line up at the Longmont Creamery to deliver milk, while cans of milk are being loaded onto the train. —Colorado Historical Society

As soon as transportation improved, prices started going down.

Transportation

Transportation was important to the growth of any Colorado community. All goods had to be hauled by freighters in the beginning. Large wagons transported supplies to Denver, where they were put into smaller wagons to be hauled into the mountains. Sometimes mules and burros carried supplies to the more isolated districts. All these transportation costs were added to the price of everything else. The town that was located on a main transportation route held an advantage over all its rivals.

The fastest way to reach Colorado before the railroad came was by stagecoach. The swaying stage crossed the plains in ten to twelve days, but the cost was high, $100 to $125 one way in 1859–60. And they weren't much fun to ride. Mark Twain recalled his trip in 1861:

> Our coach was a great swinging swaying stage, of the most sumptuous description—an imposing cradle on wheels. It was drawn by six handsome horses . . . We changed horses every ten miles, all day long, and fairly flew over the hard, level road. We jumped out and stretched our legs every time the coach stopped . . . .
>
> As the sun went down and the evening chill came on, we made preparation for bed. We stirred up the hard leather letter-sacks, and the knotty canvas bags of printed matter . . . We stirred them up and redisposed them in such a way as to make our bed as level as possible.

The stage rolled on through dust, rain, cold, and heat. The passengers ate and washed at stations along the way, while the horses were being changed and a new driver perhaps took the reins.

It is easy to understand why the railroad was preferred over the slow, tiring, four-to-six-week trip by wagon or the faster but more expensive stagecoach. Even so, until the 1870s, Colorado depended on these wagons and stages to bring supplies and people to the territory. That was one reason the settlers worried so much about the Indians. When trouble with Indians broke out and the overland trails were closed, Colorado could face food shortages, and travel back and forth to the states might be stopped.

These pioneers also enjoyed learning about what was happening in the rest of the United States, especially in their former homes. From the time of their first appearance in 1859, stages carried the mail, but people wanted even faster communication. Faster service was first supplied by the exciting Pony Express. Its route went past Julesburg and on west. The letters it brought were sent from Julesburg to Denver and the mountain towns by stagecoach. Although it seems very romantic to think of these young men riding horses carrying the mail, this method proved to be too costly. The overland telegraph replaced the Pony Express in 1861. Finally, in 1863, a branch line crossed the sage hills from Julesburg to Denver, and the clacking of the telegraph keys tied Colorado to the East Coast within minutes. Coloradans were no longer isolated.

Newspapers

Every town needed a newspaper to print local news and promote local events and businesses. To be without one was almost as bad as being bypassed by the railroad. Newspapers came early: William Byers started the *Rocky Mountain News* in April 1859. Byers beat a competitor by minutes in getting the first paper on the streets for sale. The newspaper editors of these years were often picturesque characters, and sometimes they had to fight to protect freedom of the press. One of the most fascinating was David Day of Ouray. He loved to poke fun at rival newspapers and towns, and his wit and clever writing made his *Solid Muldoon* just about the best paper in Colorado during the 1880s. Farther south, Caroline Romney edited the *Durango Record*. She pushed for reform in her community, defied outlaws, and encouraged women to come settle there to help make Durango a more civilized community. Caroline Romney proved to be a very good newspaper editor, and she helped her town get off to a fine start.

Women

Especially during the 1860s and 1870s many more men lived in Colorado than women. Caroline Romney was right—Colorado needed more women. Those who came were recognized as hardy pioneers. They found life full of hard work, trouble, and sorrows. Augusta Tabor remembered her first experience in Colorado in June 1859. While passing through Denver, her party stopped near future Golden. Her husband Horace and the other men then went on into the mountains to prospect. Augusta stayed behind and described her circumstances:

> Leaving me and my sick child in the 7 x 9 tent, that my hands had made, the men took a supply of provisions on their backs, a few blankets, and bidding me be good to myself, left on the morning of the glorious Fourth. How sadly I felt, none but God, in whom I then firmly trusted, knew. Twelve miles from a human soul save my babe.

Augusta lived through this experience and labored twenty years in Colorado before she and Horace made their fortune.

Of course, most women and their families were not so fortunate as the Tabors. Anne Ellis's mother found neither fame nor fortune in Colorado, as the daughter tells in this excerpt from her book, *The Life of an Ordinary Woman*:

> Mama never went to school a day in her life, and it was always a great sorrow to her that she could neither read nor write . . . .
>
> This is the summer before Frank is born (yes, I know I am having a baby in every chapter, but that is the way we had them!). Mama, keeping up her laundry work, still finds time to go after wild raspberries, four or five miles to the nearest patch. Here she picks all day, coming home at night so tired . . . . In addition to the laundry, Mama sewed for the men.

Anne's mother worked hard all her life in a number of mining camps. Her family never seemed able to escape its poverty.

Being a housewife and mother was an all-day job. Cooking took a lot of time, with only a wood or coal stove and no instant, prepared, or frozen foods. Then clothes had to be made or mended, washed, and ironed; homes needed to be cleaned and the shopping done. Larger families in those days meant that there were usually children to be tended to and illnesses to be treated.

There were not many jobs or professions open to women. Caroline Romney, the newspaper editor, was an exception. So was former slave Aunt Clara Brown, who, hardworking and thrifty, toiled for years as a laundress. She became a respected Central City citizen and businesswoman. Aunt Clara used some of her earnings to help other blacks migrate to Colorado and the West.

Women dominated the teaching profession but were found only occasionally in other occupations. Society of that day did not think women should be in the business world. Politics was another area believed to be unsuitable for women's involvement. They were not even allowed to vote in Colorado elections until 1894. Even at that late date, Colorado was only the second state to give them the right to vote, and it would not be until 1920 that they could vote in a presidential election.

Although women were respected and honored, they were not considered equal with men in the nineteenth century. Neither in jobs nor wages did they have equal opportunities. Fortunately, they had equal access to education, and some women worked very hard to gain total equality for their sex.

DID YOU KNOW:

- That in 1899 wages averaged as follows:
  Teachers (men), monthly $82.30
  Teachers (women), monthly $58.21
  Railroad engineers, monthly $130
  Nurses, per day $3.25
  Newspaper reporters, per week $15
  Carpenters, per day $3.00
  Bartenders, per week $23.50

Schools and Churches

Both young boys and girls went to school. Many only finished a few grades, and very few went beyond the eighth. Boys often went to work by the time they reached their mid-teens, and girls had by then reached an age when they were seriously thinking of getting married.

Edwina Fallis recalled vividly her first day at the Broadway School (now the site of the Colorado Heritage Center) in Denver in the 1880s: "Mama took me to school on the first day to tell the teacher who I was and to tell me what to do and what not to do. The do's were only two. 'Be good and mind the teacher.' " The Broadway School was a large building with a classroom for each grade. Many Colorado schools crowded everyone together in only one room, from youngsters aged six or seven to those of fifteen and sixteen. Elizabeth Amelia Lee, who was born in Caribou in 1876, went to a one-room school; the school year was sometimes three months, sometimes nine. The teachers stressed the three "R's"—reading, 'riting, and 'rithmetic. There were no "extras," just the basics. Elizabeth thought she got a good education for the time and fondly remembered her school days years later.

Students from first through eighth grade attended this one-room school at Sugarloaf above Boulder. One teacher taught them all. Most students went to work instead of going on to high school.
—*Colorado Historical Society*

The schoolhouse often became the center of community life. School Christmas programs brought people together there. Schools also hosted town meetings and guest speakers, since they were the only places large enough to hold a crowd. They could also be converted into a theater or church when necessary. A community wanted to have a school as soon as possible, because a school meant that culture had arrived, even in the most isolated of Colorado settlements.

The church building also meant that civilization had taken root, and ministers came to Colorado almost on the heels of the original miners. They came first to the settlements to preach, then they set up "circuits" to travel from district to district. John Dyer's circuit in 1861 took him back and forth across the mountains from South Park to the Gunnison country. In his first four months of preaching he walked over 500 miles. During the winter, the energetic Dyer occasionally used skis (they were called snowshoes then) to reach some of his scattered Methodist congregations, as well as to carry the United States mail. Ministers had to be hardy individuals in those days.

In the early years of mining camps, when people were moving frequently, it was better not to try to build a church. The camp could be abandoned before it was finished! Presbyterian George Darley, one of the pioneers into the San Juan mining district in the mid-1870s, explained why this kind of ministry required a special type of person. After traveling over steep mountain trails to reach a camp, he found that the only building large enough for a church service was the saloon.

> It was not always an easy matter to stop the games; winners were usually willing, while the losers were not. But so soon as the games closed then "roulette," "keno," "poker," and "faro" would give place for a time to the Gospel.
> A more convenient pulpit than a "faro-table" could not be found; nor a more respectful and intelligent audience.

Although the ministers were almost always men, women formed the real backbone of the local church. Here was an institution in which they could hold office, serve on committees, and play an active leadership role. They proved especially adept at raising money by serving dinners and organizing fairs. The church was also one of the few acceptable social outlets for them. Often the congregation and minister also led the fight to reform the town's morals, by closing the saloons and gambling "hells," among other things.

Leisure Time

Even though most men worked a five-and-a-half or six-day week during the years before 1900, they still found time to relax. Most of the leisure activities were adapted to masculine interests and tastes. Women and children had to create their own entertainment through the home or the church.

The saloons and gambling halls that Darley mentioned were for men exclusively, as were dance halls. Any women seen in them were thought to be wicked. To be sure that youngsters were not admitted, city ordinances prohibited them from visiting such places. Young children also had to be home by the time the curfew bell rang in many communities or the local policeman would escort them to their parents' house.

Much of the entertainment for families took place in the home, and might involve family members reading to one another from a book or newspaper, playing games, or just talking. Picnics and fishing trips were popular in the summer, and in the winter a sled was great for coasting down a long hill. Church and school programs were family affairs, as was an occasional play. Only a few towns had opera houses, so traveling theater companies had to improvise as best they could when performing in a hall or school. An evening at the "theater" was one to be remembered.

Christmas, New Year's, and July Fourth were the big holidays. The Christmas season featured special church and school activities, and Santa Claus always came to delight the youngsters. Santa was not a fat, jolly individual in those days; in fact, he was rather lean. Christmas trees gradually appeared in homes, but a community tree in the school or church was more common. For the adults, fancy dinners and dances highlighted the season. The dances might go on until the wee hours of the morning, with a dinner served at midnight.

How would you have liked to ride one of these big wheelers? These are the members of the "Ramblers" bicycle club as they stopped in Golden after riding over from Denver in 1886.
—Colorado Historical Society

July Fourth was a very patriotic celebration, with speeches, reading of the Declaration of Independence, and maybe a parade. Firecrackers banged all day and a baseball game might be the feature of the afternoon. A dinner and dance concluded the festivities. Baseball was by far the favorite sport of the era. Communities prided themselves on the success of their teams.

July 4, 1876 was a particularly noteworthy occasion— Colorado had just overwhelmingly voted to become a state. Lake City's *Silver World*, July 8, hailed the outcome: "Three Cheers for the State of Colorado." Since the mid-1860s people had worked hard to gain this honor, and now it was at hand. On August 1, 1876, President Ulysses Grant issued the proclamation of statehood from the White House. Colorado had become a state the year the United States celebrated its centennial. This is why it was nicknamed the Centennial State.

Fear of fire was always great in Colorado's communities. Denver's fire department is not answering a call in this photo, but seems instead to be taking part in some celebration.
—Colorado Historical Society

Urban Colorado

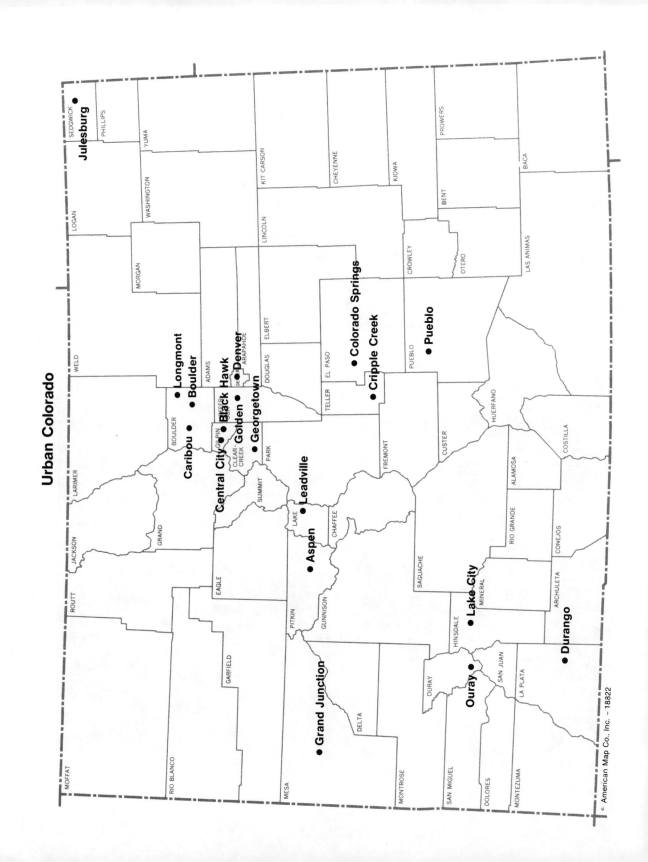

© American Map Co., Inc. – 18822

Lawlessness

Sometimes life in the towns and camps was disrupted by lawlessness, but not as much as you might have been led to believe by the movies and television. Criminals and others were attracted to frontier Colorado because there was money to be had. Law and order were slow to develop, which led to some trouble in the early mining camp days. The problem was particularly bad in a booming, wealthy community like Leadville. Newspaper editor Carlyle Davis wrote about it:

> For a number of years nothing was so cheap in Leadville as human life. Nor was the murderous instinct confined to the lower and less cultivated element . . . The bars were down and free rein was given to promiscuous bloodletting. The history of crime easily would fill a large volume.

Fictional accounts of frontier lawlessness have filled many large volumes. The most common problem any lawman had to deal with, however, was controlling the overpopulation of dogs and drunks.

Before long, law and order came to every Colorado community and county. It was bad for a community's reputation to have "a man for breakfast every morning," as some of them claimed. Most of the people wanted a peaceful atmosphere, which would attract families and investors and promote growth. They prevailed.

QUESTIONS:

1. Why was transportation so important to the growth of any Colorado community?

2. Denver became Colorado's greatest city. What factors brought this about?

3. What contributions did women make in the settlement of Colorado?

4. Would you have liked to live in a nineteenth century Colorado town? Why?

ACTIVITIES:

1. Draw a map of a typical early Colorado mining town showing the various kinds of stores they needed.

2. Draw a map showing all the early trails that led to Denver and made it the most important town.

3. Once Colorado had almost 100 different railroads. Only a few are left today. Draw a map of the one that comes closest to your school.

4. In your public library, look up the first newspaper published in your town and report to your class what it said.

5. Ask your principal what the oldest school building in your community is. Tour it to see how it differs from modern schools.

Books you might enjoy:

Robert L. Brown. *Ghost Towns of the Colorado Rockies*. Caldwell: Caxton Printers, 1968. Short histories of the towns with then-and-now photographs.

Sandra Dallas. *No More Than Five in a Bed*. Norman: University of Oklahoma Press, 1967. A fun look at the old days.

Marshall Sprague. *Newport in the Rockies*. Chicago: Swallow, 1980. Colorado Springs' ups and downs.

Carl Ubbelohde, et al., *A Colorado Reader*. Boulder: Pruett, 1982. Letters, diaries, news stories from 1776 to the 1980s.

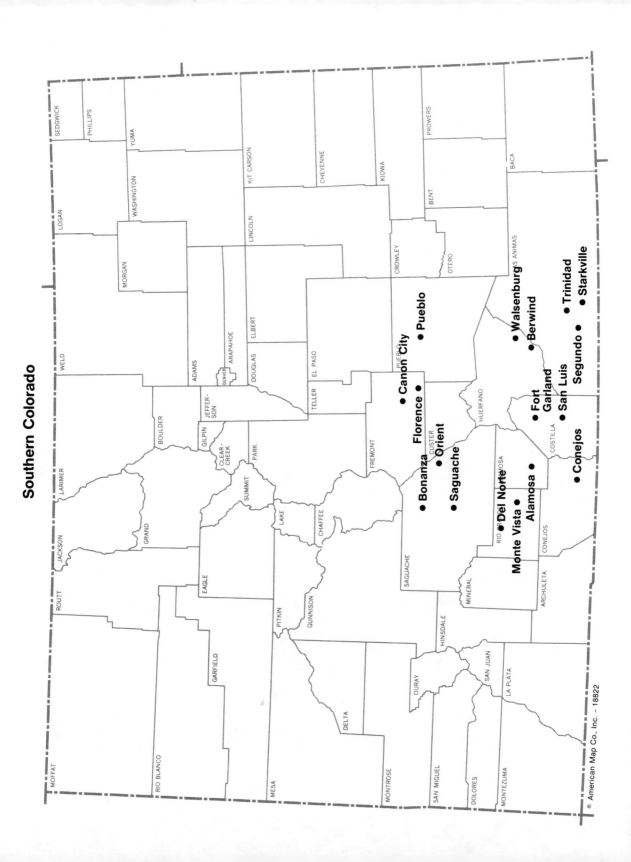

Southern Colorado

© American Map Co., Inc. – 18822

9

People of the South

The first region of future Colorado to be permanently settled was the southern San Luis Valley. Settlers from New Mexico went there in the 1850s to establish small farming settlements and a life based on their Spanish and Mexican cultures. Earlier attempts had failed, mostly because of Indian resistance—primarily from the Utes.

Settlement

The Plaza de los Manzanares was the earliest of a series of plazas or little villages in the San Luis Valley. It is now called Garcia and is located on the Colorado/New Mexico state line.

Better known is the village of San Luis (on the Culebra River) established in 1851. San Pedro, San Acacio, and Guadalupe soon followed and permanent European settlement had come to Colorado. Homes, a church, and a store were built around a central plaza or square, which became the center of community activity. Most of these people were farmers, and their farms spread out from the village, usually in long, narrow strips. Everyone lived in the village and went to work in the fields during the day.

In order for farming to survive in this semi-arid land, a source of dependable water had to be found. These people brought with them a lot of experience with irrigation, and one of their earliest projects was digging ditches to carry water to their wheat, beans, corn, and vegetables. The San Luis People's Ditch was the first water right to be recorded in Colorado, April 1852. Irrigation, which is so important to Colorado agriculture, dates from these years, as the other settlements developed their own ditch systems.

Life was not easy for people who hoped to make their homes in the San Luis Valley. They had to deal with isolation from older settlements, a harsh environment, and scarcity of water. There were also difficulties in providing enough food for their families and the worry of defending themselves against Indians. Such problems might have been enough to discourage less determined people, but these settlers stayed and built homes. To help protect them, the United States government built Fort Massachusetts in 1852. Poor planning placed it nearly fifty miles north of the settlements, however. It was the first American military establishment in Colorado. Not until 1855 did the troops bring under control the Utes and Apaches who had been raiding the region. Peace finally came to the valley. The troops remained and moved to Fort Garland in 1858, which was nearer the settlements and commanded the trails from the east over the Sangre de Cristo Mountains.

Life and Times

When the Indian threat ended, settlement spread slowly northward. Almost entirely dependent on their own resources, the settlers spun yarn and wove fabric for clothing and rugs, raised their own food, and made their own plows. Life for them developed much as it had for their parents in New Mexico. These people were Catholics, and they hoped to make the church the center of their life. This took time. First, priests from Taos, New Mexico came to conduct services and perform necessary duties, but the hopeful settlers wanted a permanent church. They got one in 1858 at Conejos, where Our Lady of Guadalupe Church was built. Catholic worship service soon became organized throughout the valley.

The church provided not only religious services, but also colorful festivals, the highlight of the year. Everyone, young and old, took part in the exciting festivities to celebrate Christmas, saints' days, weddings, and other occasions. Parades, re-

ligious plays, dances, and sports events were part of these gala affairs. They provided much needed change from the usual routine of hard work and the generally drab life that faced the settlers of the San Luis Valley.

With persistent effort, these Spanish-speaking settlers had transformed their valley by the 1860s into a place very much like their New Mexico homeland. Small plazas dotted the land, and irrigation ditches spread out from the rivers to provide the necessary moisture for the crops.

A similar pattern of settlement was developing over the mountains to the east. Along the Purgatoire River, in the valley of the same name, plazas also came into being. Settlement began ten years later (in the 1860s), and it was different because both New Mexicans and Anglos took part. Trinidad became the best known of the towns, but San Miguel Plaza, Trinchera Plaza, and others made brave attempts to attract people. Although many of these smaller settlements failed, their efforts helped others take hold and survive. The Purgatoire Valley

Our Lady of Guadalupe (at Conejos), Colorado's first church, shows Spanish influence in its architecture and adobe bricks. It looks much like the mission churches in New Mexico.
—*T.H. O'Sullivan*

combined the Spanish, Mexican, and Anglo cultures and was different in that way from the San Luis Valley, which was only Spanish/Mexican.

Arkansas Valley

To the north along the Arkansas River, small settlements came even earlier than the ones we have already discussed. A little farther down this river was the famous Bent's Fort, the scene of so much history during the fur trading days. The earliest settlements, like Bent's Fort, involved trappers and traders. One, which dated from 1842, was built on the site of what would one day be Pueblo; the name came from the trading post there. Pueblo means "town" in Spanish. Indian trader Rufus Sage described it:

> This post is owned by a company of independent traders, on the common property system, and from its situation can command a profitable trade with both Mexicans and Indians. Its occupants number ten or twelve Americans, most of whom are married to Mexican women, while everything about the establishment wears the aspect of neatness and comfort.

A Christmas Day massacre of the settlers by the Utes in 1854 ended the first period of Pueblo's history.

Thirty miles west of Pueblo, the farming settlement of San Buenaventure de los Tres Arrollos, better known as Hardscrabble, was begun in 1844. Of Hardscrabble, Sage said:

> The land indicates a fitness for agricultural purposes, and holds out strong inducements to emigrants. A small settlement of whites and half-breeds, numbering fifteen or twenty families, has already commenced . . . The only fears entertained for its success, are on account of the Indians.

With the fur trade declining, this settlement was populated almost entirely by former trappers and hunters and their families. The farms did well in wet years, but too many dry years doomed Hardscrabble. Other smaller settlements and ranches had even less distinguished careers than Hardscrabble and Pueblo.

By the time of the 1859 gold rush, the settlements on the Arkansas River were gone, except for a few ranches. The need for trading posts had ended. The little settlements had been too weak and isolated to become permanent. Poor judgment,

poor timing, hostile Indians, and bad weather ended their hopes to survive. One by one they disappeared, but for a while they had been home to the first pioneers of southern Colorado.

Growth of the San Luis Valley

The gold rush bypassed the San Luis Valley almost entirely. Several groups of prospectors tried their luck but did not find enough gold in their pans to encourage them to look further or stay long. For the farmers, life continued much as it had earlier, with one exception. Once the roads were improved, the mining camps to the north of the valley gave them a new market for their crops. Also, treaties with the Utes ended the Indians' claims to the valley, and they left the land that had been their home for so long.

Another significant change in this valley was the coming of Anglo settlers. Some went south, but most spread out into the middle and northern parts of the valley, where more land was to be found. They were farmers, too, but their settlements, like Saguache, did not look at all like the plazas to the south. They were typical frontier farming communities, like those we will discuss in a later chapter.

Around some of the major communities, squatter towns developed. Many newly-arrived immigrants settled here until they could afford better homes somewhere else. All these buildings were later torn down, and a smelter was built on this Pueblo site.
—Pueblo Library District

Finally, in the 1870s, the railroad came into the valley, end-
ing forever the frontier way of life and the isolation. The Denver
and Rio Grande came across the valley's center in 1877–78
and later extended its tracks to the north and south. Along its
lines grew such towns as Alamosa and Monte Vista; older
settlements like Del Norte prospered when the tracks reached
them. Alamosa was planned by the Denver and Rio Grande
(May 1878) and soon became the valley's most important
community. A letter writer from the new town proudly wrote
to the *Rocky Mountain News*, March 26, 1879:

> . . . not more than twenty-five miles from the city, mines are
> being opened that from indications promise to rival the best
> in this great mineral state . . . .
>
> The business houses of Alamosa are among the largest and
> best in the south. Alamosa has two newspapers, both spicy
> sheets . . . .

Such pride was not uncommon for all towns in these years.
Nearly every young community thought it had the best stores,
the best newspapers, and the brightest future.

The mines near Alamosa were located at Summitville. In
1879 they looked as if they could become some of Colorado's
great gold mines. But, as it turned out, they did not have that
much gold and were nearly mined out within a decade. Although close to Alamosa, Summitville was really part of the
San Juan mining district. The mountains that surrounded the
valley contained many such mining districts. A girl named
Anne Ellis recalled Bonanza, located to the north of Saguache:

> Bonanza was not as rough and tough as most new camps,
> because in the very beginning it was incorporated as a city,
> and always had all the town officials. In speaking of the
> population, you didn't count people, anyway, you counted
> saloons and dance-halls. There were thirty-six saloons and
> seven dance-halls.

One of the most interesting of the mining districts was Orient,
across the valley, where iron ore was mined for nearly forty
years beginning in 1880.

Mining helped settle and develop the San Luis Valley, but
it was and still is primarily agricultural. More typical than
Bonanza or Orient was Monte Vista, which dated from 1884.
A law-abiding community from the beginning, it took pride
in 1886 in having no "gambling dens or liquor saloons."

Around it developed farms and ranches, the heart of the San
Luis Valley's economy.

Pueblo

Most of the iron ore from Orient was sent to Pueblo, where
smelters and the forerunner of today's Colorado Fuel, Iron,
and Steel used it. Pueblo, built on the site of the old trading
post, grew to become southern Colorado's leading city and
the state's industrial heart. Pueblo proudly called itself the
"Pittsburgh of the West."

Reestablished in 1860, Pueblo grew slowly at first, then it
acquired two railroad connections in the 1870s—the Denver
and Rio Grande and the Santa Fe. Along with the railroads
came increased settlement and more industry. Pueblo's future
was secure. William Jackson Palmer and his fellow railroad
investors played a major role in the community's economic
development, just as they did in other towns the Denver and

*Colorado's industrial heart
was the CF&I plant in Pueblo.
These freighters were probably
involved in helping to build the
plant, only partly finished at
this moment.*
—Pueblo Library District

A fancy banquet was held in Pueblo's Mineral Palace. What do you suppose these peope ate while standing up? King Coal and Queen Silver preside from the background. —Pueblo Library District

Rio Grande reached. They decided to build an iron and steel works on their land in South Pueblo.

Pueblo was selected because it had good transportation. The railroad could easily bring in raw materials and coal and take the finished products out to many markets. Both water and land were also abundant. These men did not overlook the fact that once the steel mill got started, their railroad would make more money, and the local land they owned would increase in value. For the same reasons, Pueblo was selected for smelters in the 1880s, once Leadville and other silver districts went into full production. All this industry made Pueblo's population jump from 666 in 1870 to over 24,000 by 1890. By then it was the second largest city in the state.

Pueblo's merchants were justly proud of their city. To honor their community and the state's main industry, mining, they decided to build a "Mineral Palace." It opened in July 1890,

not quite so grand as originally planned, but a fine tribute to the town and state. Coloradans were already trying to put their best foot forward to attract tourists; Pueblo was determined not to be a step behind the others.

James Owen grew up in Pueblo in the 1870s and 1880s, and he recalled another side of community life:

> After the steel works were built, on paydays we occasionally had a rough time. One of the best fights I ever saw was between the town marshal and a big husky steelworker. The steelworker was big and strong, but the marshal was gritty . . . . they fought rough and tumble for half an hour . . . [the marshal] finally knocked the steelworker out by bumping his head on the ground, and dragged him off to the calaboose.

Coal Mining

One reason Pueblo grew to be an industrial center was because of the coal mines located in what became known as the southern coal field. Trinidad and Walsenburg were in the heart of this district. Coal mining played a very important role in nineteenth century Colorado, even though it was overshadowed by the more glamorous gold and silver mining excitements.

One of the desperate needs of early settlers was fuel. The obvious answer was wood, and the fifty-niners and their followers cut down trees recklessly. The price of wood quickly rose as the nearby forests disappeared. In the Denver/Boulder area coal outcroppings were found as early as 1859. Settlers in need of fuel simply backed their wagons up to them, chipped off enough for their use, and drove away. It was not long before some enterprising men claimed this coal for themselves and started to mine. In 1861 coal was sold in Denver and thus began Colorado's coal industry.

When coal had to be carried over long distances by wagon, however, the price became too high. The coal industry needed the railroad for two reasons: one, to ship coal more cheaply, and, two, to purchase coal to run its locomotives. Not until the railroad came did coal mining really prosper. In the 1870s and 1880s coal was found throughout much of the state, from Durango and Grand Junction on the west to Crested Butte in the mountains, and in the more famous northern and southern fields along the eastern foothills. The railroad companies eventually came to own most of the coal mines. It was in their interest to control this source of fuel, and they enjoyed the steady profits that coal shipments gave them. Southern Colorado coal soon was used to heat local homes and businesses and to power industry and smelters. It was shipped beyond the state to western Kansas and Nebraska and as far as Texas.

Coal mining was different from placer and hard rock mining. First, there were no exciting "rushes" to open coal districts; they were developed by businessmen and companies that quickly gained control of the coal mines. Because it was not as glamorous nor initially as valuable as gold and silver, coal development had to wait for population and industrial growth and improved transportation. Furthermore, coal mining was much more dangerous. The mines often were filled with gas and dust, which could explode or ignite and cause terrible accidents. A true hard rock miner did not wish to work in a coal mine—it was too dangerous, too hard, and earned him

Coal miners and their mule are ready to begin another long, dirty, tiring shift. Notice their tools and the lack of hard hats and other safety equipment.
—Colorado Historical Society

too little money. Miners were paid by the tons of coal they mined, rather than by the day.

Life in the Coal Camps

What really set the coal mines and camps apart was the fact that they were company controlled almost from their birth. That meant there was none of the freedom and individual effort that were typical of the hard rock districts and camps. The company controlled the life of the miners—it told them how much they were paid and where they could dig coal in the mine. The company owned large pieces of land around the mines for future expansion, and they ruled it like a small kingdom.

The coal camps were not like the hard rock ones. Barron Beshoar, in his book *Out of the Depths*, described the coal camps and their people:

> They lived in wretched, isolated camps strung along the slopes of twisting canons on either side of the coal mine with its unpainted shafthouse, breaker buildings and powerhouse. The single men lived in company-owned boarding houses and those with families in company-owned houses and shanties, barren little homes that reared their weatherbeaten boards above piles of ashes and tins.

The company owned the store, the homes of the miners, and the boarding house. It furnished a company doctor, perhaps a hospital, and might have the final say as to what churches would be allowed in the community and who would teach in the school. One miner was moved to say that the company owned you from birth to grave. Some companies even paid their miners in scrip, a form of paper money that had to be traded at the company store. Of course, everyone had to pay whatever prices the company charged. It was not a good situation for the miners. Labor unions, which tried to organize the workers and fight for better conditions, were often chased away by the mining companies.

Who worked in the coal mines then? Right from the start it was a different racial and cultural population from the gold and silver communities. Many of the miners came from an eastern European or Spanish/Mexican background; a few were Orientals, and only a scattering came from northern Europe, where many of the hard rock miners were born. Residents of coal communities like Hastings, Berwind, Segundo, and Starkville came from many different backgrounds. These camps developed in isolation from the rest of Colorado. Most Coloradans had no idea of what was happening in them, or how the companies controlled people's lives in the southern coal fields. This was tragic, because the seeds for much future trouble were being planted.

What Coloradans wanted was to have that coal keep coming, and it did. By 1889 2 1/2 million tons were being mined, which was wonderful, since coal production helped strengthen Colorado's economy. What people did not notice that same year was that twenty-four miners had lost their lives in various accidents in the state's coal mines. Back in January 1884, a gas and dust explosion at Crested Butte killed fifty-nine miners. Coloradans were shocked, but little or nothing was done to improve safety conditions in the coal mines. To make safety improvements would complicate mining and raise the price of coal. Conditions got worse instead of better. Colorado would pay a terrible price for its neglect. Colorado's coal miners worked and died in the dark, dangerous, dusty silence of their mines. They had no political voice or power to stand up for their rights.

Oil

Southern Colorado offered one other hope for the future—oil. During all the excitement of the early 1860s, an oil well had been drilled successfully near Canon City. This was only five years after the first commercial oil field opened in the United States (1859). For Canon City, oil was a product that came before its time. Poor transportation, extremely small market potential, lack of money, and isolation killed the oil industry before it got started.

The Florence Field, a short way down the Arkansas River from Canon City, proved more lasting and was the only producing Colorado oil field in the 1880s and 1890s. Kerosene and fuel oil were the principal products, and the town of Florence became the center of a small boom, complete with oil refineries. What the oil business really needed was the invention of the automobile!

DID YOU KNOW:

- That in 1888 you would have paid these prices to start a garden:

  package of carrot seeds, 5¢

  package of peas, 10¢

  package of tomato seeds, 15¢

  one rose bush, 20¢

  five strawberry plants, 50¢

QUESTIONS:

1. Match the following:

   San Luis Valley   a. Colorado's industrial heart

   Plazas   b. a key factor in Colorado's growth

   Denver & Rio Grande   c. site of early oil discoveries
     Railroad

   Company town   d. settlements in the coal districts

   Pueblo   e. small villages

                              f. site of the first settlements

                              g. famous tourist center

2. Why was the growth of the San Luis Valley so slow until the 1870s?

3. How did coal mining differ from hard rock mining?

4. Describe life in the 1850s and 1860s in the farming villages of the southern San Luis Valley.

ACTIVITIES:

1. Draw a map of the Rio Grande and put in the Spanish named towns that grew up along it.

2. See if there is a Catholic Church near you which has services in Spanish. Organize a class trip to these services.

3. Draw a map of the Arkansas River and put in all the towns along it.

4. Make a list of Hispanic contributions to Colorado.

5. Ask the Colorado Bureau of Mines, 1313 Sherman St., Denver, CO 80202 to give you information on Colorado's coal mine accidents.

Books you might enjoy:

Robert Adams. *The Architecture and Art of Early Hispanic Colorado.* Boulder: Colorado Associated University Press, 1974. Photographs of the Hispanic period.

Anne Ellis. *Life of an Ordinary Woman.* Lincoln: University of Nebraska, 1980 (reprint). What it was like to grow up in Bonanza and marry a miner.

Virginia M. Simmons. *The San Luis Valley.* Boulder: Pruett, 1979. The best history of this little-appreciated valley.

P.R. Griswold. *Colorado's Loneliest Railroad: The San Luis Southern.* Boulder: Pruett, 1980. For the railroad buff; lots of photographs.

Eastern Colorado

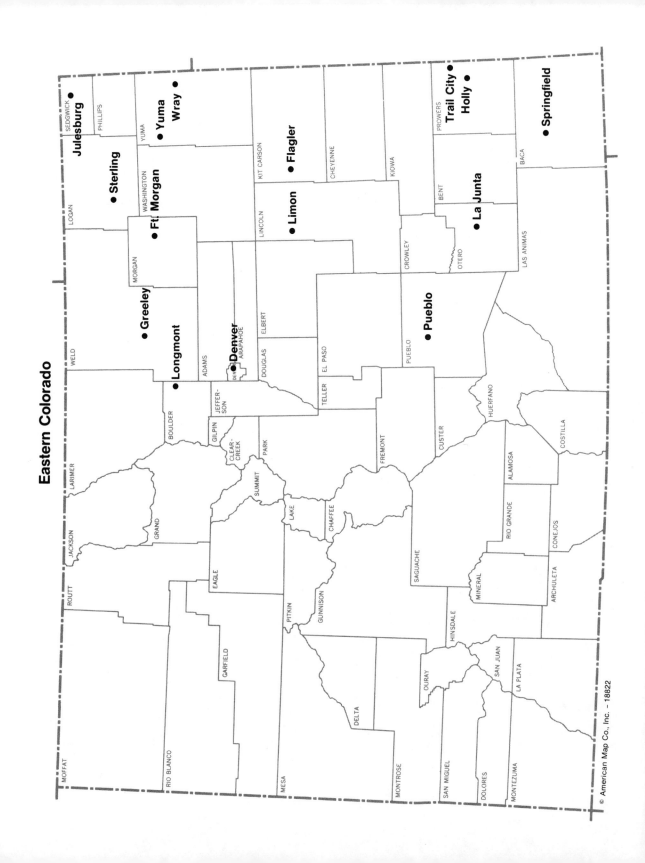

SEDGWICK

● Julesburg

PHILLIPS

● Sterling

LOGAN

YUMA

● Yuma

Wray ●

WASHINGTON

● Ft. Morgan

MORGAN

● Greeley

WELD

● Longmont

BOULDER

LARIMER

JACKSON

ROUTT

GRAND

GILPIN

CLEAR CREEK

JEFFER-SON

● Denver
ARAPAHOE
DENVER

ADAMS

PARK

SUMMIT

EAGLE

PITKIN

LAKE

CHAFFEE

GUNNISON

ELBERT

DOUGLAS

LINCOLN

KIT CARSON

● Flagler

CHEYENNE

● Limon

KIOWA

EL PASO

TELLER

FREMONT

CUSTER

SAGUACHE

HINSDALE

● Pueblo

PUEBLO

CROWLEY

OTERO

● La Junta

BENT

LAS ANIMAS

PROWERS

● Trail City

Holly ●

BACA

● Springfield

HUERFANO

ALAMOSA

COSTILLA

RIO GRANDE

MINERAL

CONEJOS

ARCHULETA

OURAY

SAN JUAN

LA PLATA

DELTA

MONTROSE

SAN MIGUEL

DOLORES

MONTEZUMA

MESA

GARFIELD

RIO BLANCO

MOFFAT

—10—
The Cowboy and the Farmer

I'm up in the morning before daylight,
Before I sleep the moon shines bright.

That is how a favorite cowboy song, "The Old Chisholm Trail," describes the work day of one of the West's most popular characters. The cowboy has ridden the range in Colorado since 1859, although today you will find him more often in a pickup truck than on a horse.

The cowboy and his horse, the ranch, the long cattle drives, and the cattle towns have become part of American history and folklore. Hardly a week goes by without an old movie or television program about the cowboy's West. Colorado was, and still is, a major part of this story.

Cattle were driven from Texas to the Pike's Peak country in 1859 because there was a good market for beef in the mining districts. Several of the cattle trails, including the Dawson and Goodnight-Loving, came into Colorado. The longhorns were driven over these hot, dusty, dangerous trails by the cowboys. The first ranches were started because the miners wanted meat. The eastern plains of Colorado had once been called the "great American desert," but cattlemen found the grass very nourishing for their cattle. For that reason they established their ranches on the plains and not in the mountains. The range was open and free for anyone who had the courage to risk the hard life of ranching.

Open Range

The great days of ranching were called the open range era. It lasted only about twenty years, from 1865 to the mid-1880s. Coloradans had to wait until the Cheyenne and Arapaho Indians were removed from the eastern plains and the railroad arrived before they could fully enter into the cattle business. Once they started, the industry boomed here as it did in Texas, Wyoming, and Montana. By the mid-1870s Denver was becoming the center of the livestock industry. Denver's railroad connections and stockyards made it a logical place to buy, sell, and ship cattle to meat markets and cattle buyers.

Operating a ranch looked easy and, in some ways, it was. All you needed at first were cattle, cowboys, and a branding iron. The grass and water were free. No one else wanted to live on the prairies of eastern Colorado at that time. The cattle were turned loose to graze on the open range. Once or twice a year they were rounded up, branded, and driven to market or to the railroad's loading pen. Each ranch burned its own brand into its cattle and calf hides for easy identification.

The ranch itself had only a couple of quickly constructed buildings and a corral. Not much money was spent on them. Horses were not too expensive to buy. Wages for the cowhands, or "hands," as they were called, were another expense. Their pay averaged about $30 a month, plus room and board. A top hand might receive as much as $45. The number of cowboys that were needed changed with the seasons. More were required in the summer and during roundups and drives, but only a few in winter. Extra seasonal hands were called waddies.

"Grass is King" described the days of the open range. The cattle grazed on free grass and multiplied naturally. All the owner had to do was round them up, brand them, and sell them for a profit. Grass and cows were the road to fortune. No one in Colorado became more famous or wealthy by following this road than John Wesley Iliff.

*John Wesley Iliff, Colorado's nineteenth century cattle king.
—Colorado Historical Society*

John Wesley Iliff

John Wesley Iliff was no ordinary cattleman. He ran his cattle across a range that stretched more than 100 miles west from Colorado's eastern border and ran 60 miles north and south, over 650,000 total acres. His chief ranch headquarters were 40 miles from Julesburg. Northeastern Colorado was his range. Iliff did not own all of this land, but he controlled the water. That meant the land was his to use, because without water the land was useless for other ranchers.

Twenty-eight-year-old Iliff had come to Colorado in the gold rush of 1859 and opened a store in Denver. He soon realized that there was a lot of money to be made in the cattle business, so he invested in a herd of cattle. Within ten years Iliff was purchasing 10,000 to 15,000 Texas longhorns each spring at $10 to $15 each. He fattened them on his range for a year or two and then sold them for $30 to $50. He hired about forty hands in the summer and about twelve in the winter to herd his cattle. Iliff became a rich and powerful man in Colorado.

By the 1870s, however, he realized that the days of the open range would not last forever. Farmers were moving onto the plains, and towns were being built where there had once been only open space and cattle. Iliff also understood that the ranching methods in use then were not the best. He began to make changes. For example, he brought in better breeds of cattle. Longhorn meat was tough and stringy; Shorthorn and Hereford meat was much better. Ranchers had been losing a third or more of their herds during the storms and harsh weather of winter by letting the cattle graze on their own. Iliff decreased these losses by building shelters for his animals and by cutting hay for winter feed. He used sound business practices to run his ranch and refused to borrow money. Iliff was one of the first to understand that the range could be overgrazed by too many cattle. He worked hard to keep it free from overcrowding and disease.

John Iliff was one of the most advanced cattlemen of his time. After the open range ended, people realized that he had introduced scientific ranching, the basis of today's industry. Iliff died in February 1878, and his widow eventually donated part of his fortune to establish the Iliff Seminary at the University of Denver, a rather unusual monument for a cattleman. One of his friends paid him this tribute: "He was the squarest man that ever rode over these Plains."

End of the Open Range

Iliff was right, the days of the open range would soon end. The coming of the farmer hurt; so did overgrazing the land and crowding too many cattle onto the range. Too much debt and poor management put ranchers on shaky ground by the mid-1880s. Then came some unusually harsh years, 1885–1887, that brought drought and terrible winters. Cattle died by the thousands. Panicked owners shipped what they could and flooded the market. The price for cattle collapsed. Finally, all that poor management and borrowing to buy more cattle caught up with the ranchers. The days of the open range ended.

In their place came ranching based on better breeds of cattle, fenced pastures, winter feeding, and more businesslike methods. Grass was no longer king, but the cattle industry now had a more solid foundation. By 1900 cattle were being raised from the eastern plains to the mountain valleys and in the far western parts of the state. Cattle raising had become one of the most important industries in Colorado's economy.

Before it disappeared, however, the open range left behind the legend of the cattle frontier. Colorado even claimed to have one real cattle town, like the more famous Dodge City, Kansas. This was Trail City, six miles north of Holly on the Kansas border. It was established in 1884 but lasted only about six years. Located on the National Cattle Trail, Trail City was a place where cowboys could "let off steam" after driving the herds up from Texas. But the days of the long drive and open range soon came to an end, and so did Trail City's reason for being.

Cowboys

The hero of this time in history was the cowboy. His life has been made to look exciting in books and movies. Was it really like that? Jack Keppel did not think so. He came to eastern Colorado in 1887 and worked on a ranch. Jack was a "greenhorn" who didn't even know how to ride a horse. His pay came to $15 a month. In the summer of 1889, it was raised to $20. He learned to do all the ranch chores after a while, except milking cows, and he said he was "not good at that." Jack had difficulties getting used to washing with and drinking alkali water. It tasted terrible (salty), and too much

of it could cause illness. Like most cowboys, he drifted from place to place and worked for several ranchers before homesteading his own little ranch/farm. There was not much excitement or glamour in Jack's life. Mostly it was just plain hard work and a "very lonesome" existence.

Still, the cowboy's life was not all work and no play. When the cowboy went to town, he could have some fun. Sometimes he got too rowdy, as in this story of a Denver accident. Two cowboys, who were racing their broncos, crashed into a trolley car and

> . . . smashed three of the roof supports, splintering the seats and breaking down the grip guard. One rider went hurtling through the car like a human cannon ball, and landed on all fours in the street on the other side. . . . His companion struck the side of the car and bounced back into the roadway. Marvelous to relate neither were hurt [nor any passengers].

In 1894 Perry Davis helped drive some horses from South Dakota to Texas. He and his friends had to deal with dangerous river crossings, quicksand, unruly livestock, rapid weather

Without cowboys, neither Iliff nor any other cattleman could have managed his ranch. These fellows don't look like the Hollywood version.
—*Colorado Historical Society*

changes, and many other problems before they reached the end of the trail. While they were crossing eastern Colorado, Davis wrote in his diary on September 17:

> Pulled through long lane. Horses tore down wire fences; got badly cut and went through brush. Didn't pay for fences. Moved eight miles from Platte and camped for noon. Move about eight miles after dinner and water in Beaver [Creek] and pull into the hills a couple of miles and camp. Sheep here; feed short. See sand lizards; poison. Horses run into two bands of sheep, stampede.

All in all, it doesn't sound like much fun, does it? Being a cowboy was hard work.

Sheep

Cattlemen did not like sheep as a rule. Sometimes the sheep scared their horses, as Davis wrote in his diary. Both the cowboys and the sheepherders wanted the same range for their animals, and cowmen believed the legend that cattle would not eat where sheep had grazed.

Although the sheep had come before the cattle—New Mexico settlers in the San Luis Valley had brought them north—sheep raising grew slowly. Not until the 1870s and 1880s did it spread very far. Troubles came quickly and lasted a long time. For almost forty years the cattlemen and sheepmen fought one another for the mountain valleys and river bottoms. Sometimes these fights became violent. In March 1877 a flock of 1,600 sheep was poisoned and clubbed to death near Pueblo as a warning to sheepmen to keep out of the area. These "cattle-sheep wars" also extended to Colorado's Western Slope. Finally, common sense brought an end to the struggle. This tragic period in Colorado agricultural history brought no credit to those who used violence to keep someone else from making a living.

DID YOU KNOW:

- That in the 1890s the following cost:
  a well broken saddle horse $50–$60
  a saddle $15
  men's blue denim overalls 50¢
  steel plow (horse-drawn) $9.75
  a pocket watch $1.68

Farming

A much greater threat to the cattleman was the farmer or homesteader. The name homesteader came from the Homestead Act, passed by Congress in 1862. This act let any American citizen, or anyone who wanted to be a citizen, choose 160 acres of public land for a farm, or homestead, as it was called. After five years of living on the land and making improvements, the homesteader was given the land. Or, after six months' residence, the land could be bought for $1.25 an acre. Homesteaders had to wait until the Indians were removed and the railroad had come before they could settle very much of the eastern plains. They arrived after the cattlemen had already gotten nicely started.

Farming had really begun much earlier than that—it had come along with the fifty-niners. The miners needed more than meat to eat, so some of the men turned to farming. They realized they could make more money by growing crops and selling them to other miners than they could by mining. They farmed along the rivers that came out of the mountains. Most of them did not have to learn any new skills, because they had been farmers back in the Midwest.

William Byers, in the very first issue of his newspaper, the *Rocky Mountain News*, told his readers that money could be made from farming. David Wall was one who took that advice. He settled in the Golden area and established a farm. His site was perfect, because he could sell his produce to both the miners in the mountains and the residents of Denver and Golden. He irrigated his crops by digging a ditch from Clear Creek. He made a nice profit until grasshoppers almost ruined him by eating his crops in 1862. Other farmers settled along the rivers and creeks in the Huerfano, Arkansas, Platte, and Boulder valleys.

Byers's dream of having homegrown products came true by the fall of 1859 in Denver, but it would be many more years before Colorado farmers could provide all the produce and grain that were needed. It took time to find out the length of the growing season, what crops could be grown successfully, and how much rainfall could be counted on during the growing season. Not only that, equipment had to be brought out to the West. Some of the common farm animals also had to be imported. "Experienced hog drivers" drove 252 hogs on a march from the Missouri River in 1861, and the first colony of bees came by wagon train the next year. The first turkeys trotted all the way to Denver, making as many as twenty-five miles a day when a tail wind helped them along.

The first farmers started their homes and farms on their own. That was the usual way on the American farming frontier. However, when the farmers moved away from the well-watered river valleys near the foothills to Colorado's eastern plains, they had to make some changes. The first thing they had to do was find water and get it to their crops. Without water, farming would fail and so would any settlement. Building an irrigation system took more money and skill than most Coloradans had in the 1860s. So they had to work together.

Colony Settlements and Water Law

The first really successful plains farmers solved some of these problems with colony settlements. Colony settlement was an interesting idea. A group of people would join together to plan a settlement and combine their skills and money. In this way they hoped to get all the needed finances, knowledge, skills, and labor to establish and maintain a town and an irrigation system. A group of farm families who moved together could also overcome the loneliness of the eastern plains. Loneliness had always been a problem on the farming frontier, especially for the women and children.

The best known of Colorado's colonies was the Union Colony, which started the town of Greeley. It was named after Horace Greeley, who helped promote it in his New York City newspaper. The Union colonists built an irrigation system and began farming. Longmont was also established using the same idea. These were the most successful of the many attempts during these years to plant colony settlements.

When the farmers began to take water out of the rivers, the question was asked, "Who has the right to use it?" There was not enough for everybody if settlements grew too fast. Because both mining and agriculture needed large amounts of water, Colorado was one of the first states to make water laws to decide how it should be used. Out of all these laws and court cases came the doctrine of prior appropriation. What this meant was "first in time, first in right"; that is, the person who had the earliest water claim (say, April 1860) had the first right to use the water. The person with the second earliest date (for instance, May 1860) came next, and so on. The persons who held water rights could not waste the water—they had to make good use of it. In water law this is called "beneficial use." Water is still important to Colorado's growth, just as it was over 100 years ago when these laws were being made.

Homesteading

Despite the success of colonies at Greeley and Longmont, most of the eastern plains were settled by individual farmers who hoped to make their fortune in this new land. They were encouraged by the railroads, which crossed the plains on their way to Denver and Pueblo. These railroads had land to sell to farmers, and they could make money by shipping the farmers' crops to market.

Imagine the plains being divided up like a giant checker board, with each section containing 640 acres (one mile square). The railroads were given every other section along their tracks. This was the land they had to sell. They used some of it to start towns, such as Wray, Ft. Morgan, and Yuma along the Burlington Railroad, or Burlington, Flagler, and Limon on the Rock Island line. The railroads offered to sell their other sections of land to farmers and ranchers.

This sod house near Merino indicates that the homestead had been built very recently. For the wife and mother, life on the farm meant long hours of work and lots of loneliness. —Colorado Historical Society

Settlers came with wonderful dreams of homesteading in eastern Colorado. What they found was quite different from what they had imagined. Trees were in short supply, so there was no wood for fuel or building. They had to construct their homes with sod cut from the soil on their farms. These houses were cheap to build and fairly warm in the winter (when heated by a stove) and cool in the summer. Cornstalks, straw, corn cobs, and even cow "chips" were used instead of wood in the stove. There were other problems, too, as is shown by this comment from Alvin Steinel's *History of Agriculture in Colorado*:

> Mush and milk was the diet that sustained many a family through the pioneering period, although those properly equipped to farm soon had a garden under way and a supply of eggs and meat coming from a flock of hens, with plenty of salt pork in prospect later. The obstacles to settlement which nature had set up in a semi-arid climate . . . were serious enough, but the problem was made doubly hard by the fact that free homesteads and cheap railroad land attracted a class of people who were generally without capital, and often without farming experience.

Most of the people stayed and tried to start a farm and home, despite all the problems.

A proud farm family near Sterling is dressed in its finest. The frame home, windmill, and nicely painted barn show they were prospering.
—Colorado Historical Society

Rainmaking

Settlers poured in and, for a while, so did the rains. A hopeful saying that rains followed the plow seemed to be true. The people didn't realize that they had settled during a wet cycle in the late 1870s and 1880s. When the dry years came, the farmers started to worry. They turned to anyone who promised to bring rain. As a result, so-called rainmakers appeared and practiced their "magic." Frank Melbourne, according to a *Denver Post* article, August 2, 1891, worked from a "mysterious little house from which the inventor controls the elements." He promised hope to eastern Colorado:

> I have passed through Colorado three months ago and made it a point to take particular notice of the country through which I passed, the weight of the air and other points which the general traveler would not notice . . . I can bring rain over an area of 250,000 square miles, and am positive I could bring it in Denver easier, than I can here [Canton, Ohio, where he was living].

The "magic" of the rainmakers did not work and in the late 1880s and 1890s much of eastern Colorado was abandoned.

Farm work demanded a great deal of physical labor by horse and men. This Hispanic farmer near Pueblo is preparing his field for planting. —Pueblo Library District

The farmers had been defeated by drought and low farm prices. Others would try their luck again after 1900. At that time they would use what became known as "dry land" farming methods.

It would take a while by the slow trial and error process for the right crops, seeds, machinery, and methods to be found. Eventually they would be, though, and agriculture would take its place as an important part of Colorado's economy.

The Grange

No matter how one looks at it, the life of the farmer was filled with hard work, drudgery, loneliness, and disappointment. The colonies made things better, but there was little help for the typical farmer. Still, one organization for farmers did make life a little easier. The Grange, or Patrons of Husbandry, had come to Colorado in the 1870s. It gave the farmers and their families social and educational opportunities by providing meetings, picnics, dances, and various publications. The Grange halls in the farming counties became social centers and places where you could learn about the latest farm machinery, stove, or cooking technique. Some of these Grange halls still exist. Is there one in your county?

County fairs were also a time for rural families to get together and a place to advertise local crops. Some towns had special days to promote themselves and their agriculture; for example, Rocky Ford had "Melon Day"; Greeley, "Potato Day"; Sterling, "Farmers' Picnic"; and Longmont, "Pumpkin Pie Day." "Lamb Day" in Fort Collins and "Pickle Day" in Platteville were some of the other harvest festivals. On the Western Slope, Grand Junction sponsors "Peach Day" and Glenwood Springs celebrates "Strawberry Day." Since 1887, Pueblo has hosted the largest agricultural festival, the Colorado State Fair. It continues to attract top crops and top country musicians.

Colorado's biggest rodeo and livestock show began in 1906. The National Western Stock Show is still held for ten days every January. Ranchers from all over North America meet in Denver to exhibit and to inspect, to buy and to sell all kinds of animals. Although the stock show traditionally happens during the coldest part of winter, hundreds of thousands come to the rodeo, the Beef Palace, and the Hall of Education, where you can see dozens of different kinds of animals, from rabbits to roosters.

QUESTIONS:

1. Why was John Wesley Iliff so important to the cattle business in Colorado?

2. Define these terms: open range, cattle-sheep wars, beneficial use, homestead, the grange.

3. Why was the life of the farmer such hard work and so lonely for his family?

4. Who do you believe is more important in Colorado's history, the cowboy or the farmer? Why?

ACTIVITIES:

1. Bring some records or tapes of cowboy songs and play them for the class. Ask your classmates how the lyrics of the song reflect the cowboy's life.

2. Visit a working ranch in your county to see how cattle are raised today.

3. As a class project for the spring, plant vegetables outside your classroom and see which ones do best in your climate.

4. Find out what fall festival has been celebrated in your community. Look up old newspapers for that time of year and see how people have celebrated this festival over the years.

5. Ask your county agricultural agent to come talk to your class about the types of farming and ranching practiced in your community.

Books you might enjoy:

Robert H. Adams. *White Churches of the Plains*. Boulder: Colorado Associated University Press, 1970. A photographic look.

Colorado Heritage (1981). Denver: Colorado Historical Society, 1981. Stories about cowboys and ranching.

Harold Hamil. *Colorado Without Mountains*. Kansas City: Lowell, 1976. The eastern plains as he remembers them while growing up there.

Maurice Frink, et al. *When Grass Was King*. Boulder: University of Colorado Press, 1956. History of John Iliff and the open range days.

The books by Laura Ingalls Wilder, though not specifically about Colorado, beautifully describe the life of the farm family.

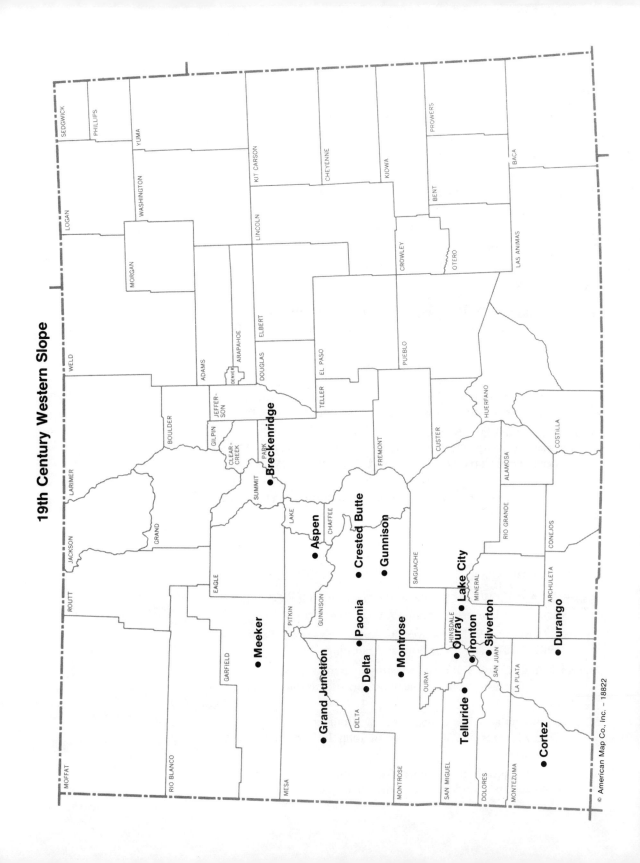

19th Century Western Slope

© American Map Co., Inc. – 18822

— 11 —
The Western Sloper

On the Pacific side of the Continental Divide in Colorado lies the Western Slope. Its high mountains, river valleys, plateaus, and lonely stretches of semideserts and deserts are some of the state's most beautiful scenery and rugged land. This part of Colorado gives birth to the great Colorado River and contains many of the state's water reserves. Water has always been important to the state's growth and development and will continue to be in the future. Water is the lifeblood of the Western Slope.

Prospecting and Placering

These lands had been home to the Indians for many, many years—first, the Basketmakers, then the Cliff Dwellers, and finally the Utes. At first, the high mountains kept the goldseekers of 1859 from invading this part of Colorado. But they could not be kept out for long, and they found passes through those mountains. By midsummer the fifty-niners had arrived on the Western Slope in their frantic search for gold. Most of them did not stay long. The loneliness, the threat of Indian attacks, transportation problems, and a hard winter drove out all but the most hardy. This would be the pattern for the next decade, while the Eastern Slope was gradually settled. Breckenridge and Summit County had the only gold placers that proved rich enough to keep miners there for a couple of years. Then they, too, declined. The problem of moving goods through the Rocky Mountains killed interest in other mining areas, such as the San Juan Mountains and the Gunnison country.

Rumors of gold and silver still found their way east, however, and continued to lure prospectors to the Western Slope. All of them thought they could unlock its mineral secrets. Settlers tried to start homes, but their job was difficult until they could earn a living and transportation improved. Miner Daniel Conner wrote about the appearance of the first woman and her daughter in the mining district of Georgia Gulch, near Breckenridge:

> She [an old lady] brought her daughter with her, whom she addressed by the affectionate sobriquet of 'Sis.' Sis was the first young lady to arrive in Georgia Gulch, and the fact that she waited upon customers gave the establishment a heavy run of business. . . . The common remark of the miners, when meeting friends, was first, 'Boys, there is a gal in the gulch.' 'When did she come?' 'Oh, I don't know, but she's there.' 'Hurrah! Hurrah for Georgia Gulch . . .'

Until more women and families arrived, the Western Slope would not have permanent settlement. As late as the mid-1870s it was still being called an "unknown land." One author boldly forecast that in time it would become "thickly settled."

Mining finally provided the solution to most of the problems. The San Juan Mountains were prospected in the 1870s. Because of the activity there, the towns of Ouray, Silverton, and Lake City came into being and provided the base for more exploring. The neighboring Gunnison country was opened in the late 1870s and the region attracted a lot of attention in the early 1880s. The town of Gunnison was the transportation and business center. North and east of it were the silver mining districts and camps.

Utes

Mining and the settlement that came with it also brought tragedy to the Western Slope, because most of it belonged to the Utes. This fact did not concern the miners and other newcomers. In 1863 and again in 1868 the United States government had promised this land to the Utes. It was to be their reservation. That seemed only fair, since it had been their home for hundreds of years. Then came the miners, who discovered and mined gold and silver. To them, it seemed unfair that the Utes should have all the land, especially since the Indians did not mine these treasures. It was the same clash of different cultures that had occurred when European settlers first came to the New World centuries before.

The Colorado conflict reached the danger point in the San Juans in the early 1870s. This was Ute land and the miners had overrun it. In 1873 the government and Utes sat down at the conference table once more. In the Brunot Treaty the Utes gave up their claim to the San Juan Mountains. The miners could now start mining legally.

But that was not enough for these new settlers. Other lands held by the Utes seemed just as attractive to the miner, town builder, rancher, and farmer. Cries that the "Utes must go" were heard throughout Colorado and especially from the Western Slope. The Utes stood in the way of "progress," as Coloradans defined it in the 1870s. They must be conquered just as the mountains had been.

Ouray

The Utes did not want to leave their homeland. Their most famous leader, Ouray, tried with all his ample skills to keep them there. Ouray was one Ute whom the white man respected. For instance, Ouray (the town named after him) held a "grand reception" for him in March 1879. Two hundred persons turned out to honor him. The local band serenaded Ouray and his wife Chipeta. The *Ouray Times,* March 15, praised this good man and hoped that he would be a "better friend than ever of the whites." Unfortunately, he could not control all of the Utes. Only six months later trouble came at the White River Agency near the present town of Meeker.

The United States Indian Agent, Nathan Meeker, a good but stubborn man, wanted the Utes to farm, something they did not want to do. When Meeker ordered the race track plowed up to stop their horse racing and betting, tempers exploded. Meeker called for help, but it came too late. In September he and eleven men were killed by the Utes. The agency's white women and children were carried off into captivity. The newspapers screamed that a "Ute War" had broken out.

The column of troops that was on the way to rescue Meeker and his co-workers had been stopped by Ute warriors. The soldiers had to be rescued before they could march on to find the sad scene at the agency. Ouray tried desperately to persuade his fellow Utes to release their prisoners to prevent a full-scale war. He succeeded, but the damage had already been done. Not even Ouray could now save the Utes' homeland for them.

Colorado's most famous Ute family, Ouray and Chipeta.
—Museum of Western
*   Colorado*

In 1880 he and other Utes traveled to Washington and signed a new agreement. This one removed all the Utes involved in the "massacre" from Colorado into eastern Utah. Only the Southern Utes, who had not participated, were allowed to stay on their reservation in what is now La Plata and Montezuma counties. The following year the Northern Utes left Colorado. In 1882 the remaining land on the Western Slope was declared open for settlement. The white settlers came on the heels of the retreating Utes.

Ouray, the wise and dedicated Ute leader, did not live to see this final tragedy in his people's Colorado story. He died in August 1880, while working for approval of the agreement. No Indian leader stands taller in the history of Colorado than Ouray. And some of his tribe, the Southern Utes and the Ute Mountain Utes, live in Colorado to this day on their two reservations in the state's southwestern corner.

Transportation

At the time of the Ute troubles, transportation improvements began to come to the Western Slope. This was the other major development necessary to open this area of Colorado completely. First came the freighter to haul goods with his freight wagons and mule or burro pack trains. One of the most famous freighters was Dave Wood, who ran his freight teams, especially in the San Juans, from the 1870s into the 1890s.

Freighters hauled an amazing variety of things. You can imagine what some of them were: ore from the mines, oats, corn, mining equipment, blasting powder, general supplies for stores, furniture, and food. They charged by the pound and worked as long as weather permitted. In the snowy winter months they used pack trains to bring supplies. This could be very dangerous because of snow slides and extreme cold. Freighting was risky in all seasons, and the best efforts did not always satisfy customers. They complained to Dave Wood about the following matters:

> Poor oats are hard to sell—please send good ones neither musty or dirty.
> We don't put ourselves up as kickers but would like to know why it is you ship freight to others for less than you do us?

18 lbs. of cheese were destroyed in one of your wagons—
got down between some barrels where got mashed and
gorged.

You must have some goods of ours that has been in your
possession a long time.

Roads now getting in fair condition. You may load and
ship our ore cabinet case, but I wish you or Mr. Marshall
would personally look after the loading of same to see that
no danger of either breaking the glass or rubbing the stand.

Dave Wood helped open the San Juans as much as any other
individual did, despite the complainers. Freighting was abso-
lutely necessary. So were the stagecoaches, which carried the
mail and passengers. The very best method, though, was the
railroad. It was faster, generally cheaper, and could be depended upon all year—usually. We have already discussed the
Denver and Rio Grande and what it did in other places in Colorado. William Jackson Palmer and his railroad had been a great
help to Leadville, Colorado Springs, Denver, and Pueblo. It
would be even more important in western Colorado. Without
the railroad, settlement could not have come so easily or covered
so much land.

Railroads

The Denver and Rio Grande's narrow-gauge rails (three feet
wide) proved to be ideal for the mountains and canyons of
the Western Slope. They were easier to build and take care of,
they could climb steeper grades up the mountains, and they
cost less than the four-foot, eight-and-a-half-inch broad gauge,
used more often throughout the United States. Palmer's railroad went everywhere in the mountains and beyond.

One branch swung south and west from Alamosa to
Durango, which the D&RG founded, and then up to Silverton.
Another crossed Marshall Pass and went to Gunnison, then
west to Montrose and Grand Junction, with other branches
eventually going to Ouray and Lake City. Rio Grande tracks
reached the booming silver camp of Aspen in the 1880s. Both
mining and farming regions were helped by rail connections.
It took hard work, money, and courage to build into these
new areas. The D&RG was not afraid to move into unexplored
territory, and everyone benefited.

Other railroads were not about to let the Rio Grande have
the Western Slope all to itself. The Denver, South Park, and

Pacific raced it to Gunnison, only to come in second. The same thing happened to the Colorado Midland going into Aspen. The road builder, Otto Mears, who had done so much to open toll roads in the San Juan region, also dabbled in railroading. He built several short lines out of Silverton to tap nearby mining districts and a longer one, the Rio Grande Southern, that stretched from Durango to Ridgway. At one time Silverton had four narrow-gauge railroads and crowed that it was the "Narrow Gauge Capital of the World."

The railroads brought growth to the mining regions, because they lowered the cost of freight and made it easier for people to reach the mountain districts. They helped the farmer and rancher for the same reasons. They also allowed them to ship their products and cattle much more easily. Railroads were important to towns, no doubt about it. A town without a railroad was considered "too dead to bury."

Tourists came too, and because of them a new industry was off to a good start. You could buy a ticket in Denver to take

Without the freighter to haul everything from pins to lumber, Colorado could not have been settled or developed. This is one of Dave Wood's outfits moving out of Telluride.
—Duane A. Smith

the "circle route." First, you would ride the Denver and Rio Grande Western, as it was renamed, all the way to Silverton. Then you would change to Mears's Silverton railroad and travel to Ironton. Here a thrilling stagecoach ride down a narrow canyon road brought you to Ouray, where you rejoined the D&RGW on the trip back to Denver. It was as much fun as it sounds. The "Rainbow Route," as it was sometimes called, carried tourists through some of the most beautiful of Colorado's mountains and canyons. The ease and comfort of travel was amazing for a state only thirty years old. Today, you can still travel by train over the Silverton-Durango and Chama-Antonito parts of the Rainbow Route.

The railroads brought some bad along with the good. In their rush to reach the Western Slope they often hurried too much. Someone said about the South Park Railroad that it was "poorly surveyed, poorly located, poorly engineered, poorly financed and in financial trouble during most of its history." So were some of the others, because it took a lot of time to reach the point where profits could be made. Western Slopers grumbled about such problems, but they could also laugh about them. D&RGW, oldtimers said, meant "Dangerous & Rapidly Growing Worse." The little Crystal River and San Juan Railroad that ran to Marble was affectionately known as the "Can't Run and Seldom Jumps."

DID YOU KNOW:

- That in Durango in 1881 you could buy:
    13 loaves of fresh bread for $1.00
    a "square meal" for 25¢ to 50¢
    one pound of sirloin steak for 10¢
    a ticket to a play for 25¢
    a daily newspaper for 5¢
    and you could rent a hotel room for $3 a day.

Hard Rock Mining

The discovery of gold and silver, removal of the Utes, and the coming of the railroads finally turned the Western Slope into a miners' delight. They scurried about the mountains looking for more minerals. Ranchers and farmers settled in the valleys, and town builders surveyed and built where the

Utes had roamed only a few years earlier. In the 1880s and 1890s the Western Slope came into its own. Colorado had a new frontier to settle.

Mining had called attention to the region in the first place. It had encouraged the railroads, settlers, and investors to come in and had advertised the Western Slope. Mining followed the same pattern in western Colorado as it had in other parts of the state. First it boomed, then it busted. Gunnison mines had their moments of excitement, then faded away. Aspen replaced Leadville as Colorado's silver queen in the late 1880s. Within ten years it, too, was declining. Then the San Juans blossomed into a major mining region. With their wealth of gold, silver, and other minerals, the San Juans continued as an important mining area. Over a hundred years later mining still goes on in the Silverton/Telluride district and on a smaller scale elsewhere.

Mining helped the farmer and rancher get started, because the miners offered high prices for their products. When mining declined, farming and tourism became the main local industries.

It would be hard to imagine anyone you know dressed as these men and women are to go fishing. Grand Lake and the Colorado mountains have been favorite tourist recreation spots for over a century now. —Colorado Historical Society

Growth

The Western Slope, because settlement began later, found itself far behind the Eastern Slope in development, population, finances, and political power. It was never able to catch up in the nineteenth century and remained a poor "country cousin" to Denver and the rest of the state. This meant it was something like being a colony of the older parts of Colorado. You may remember that the original thirteen colonies of the United States depended on England for money, trade, and manufactured products. In much the same way, the Western Slope depended on outside investors, bankers, and businessmen. This dependence created problems as the years went by.

Water would be what would cause the most trouble. Water was one thing the Western Slope had in large amounts. The Eastern Slope and nearby states needed more and more of it for their farms and towns. The Western Slope wanted to use its own water for farming, cities, and mining. Both slopes looked to the same water sources to meet their needs. Who would be allowed to use them would be the important question of the twentieth century.

By 1900, after only twenty-five years of settlement, the Western Slope had developed its own way of life, based on its many resources. Some of the problems which had held back settlement for so long had been solved. Grand Junction had 3,500 people and was well on its way to being the largest Western

Before we had refrigerators and freezers, blocks of ice kept things cool. Cutting the ice from lakes and ponds was a winter occupation. It was stored in sheds, most often with sawdust for insulation against spring and summer heat.
—North Fork Historical Society

Slope city, although it was not anywhere near Denver's 133,000. Grand Junction's peaches and apples, grown in the heart of rich agricultural land with a long growing season, were already famous. The neighboring Grand Valley had plenty of water and a mild climate and became the Western Slope center of agriculture. The development of sugar beets, which became an important crop for all of Colorado, was pioneered here. At other places, such as Durango, Cortez, Montrose, and Delta, farmers were busy raising crops, and Paonia rivaled Grand Junction in fruit growing.

Not all the Western Slope grew at the same rate. The northwestern section continued to be a frontier land for many years. Some ranchers and farmers moved into that area by 1900, but it still lacked railroads. No rich gold or silver strikes attracted the miners, and what towns there were remained very small. This was Colorado's last frontier.

The years after the early 1870s were exciting ones for Western Slopers. They saw their region opened and steadily settled. They loved their land, even with all the problems it presented. Most of them would probably have agreed with newspaperman/poet Cy Warman:

I would stand amid these mountains, with their hueless caps of snow,
Looking down the distant valley, stretching far away below;
And with reverential rapture, thank my Maker for this grand,
Peerless, priceless panorama, that a child can understand.

Students skied to school in the old days near Hahn's Peak. Notice the difference in "poles," bindings, and skiing attire. —Al Wiggins, Craig.

QUESTIONS:

1. What three factors turned the Western Slope into a "miners' delight"?

2. Identify these people: Dave Wood, Ouray, Otto Mears, and William Jackson Palmer.

3. Imagine yourself a railroad builder. Why would you want to build your railroad into the San Juans and what problems would you face?

4. You are a Ute in the 1870s; what would your reaction be to the settlement of your land?

ACTIVITIES:

1. Draw a map of Colorado on the blackboard. Then draw in the Continental Divide to show the class which part of Colorado is on the Western Slope.

2. Survey your class's attitudes by asking them whether they prefer the eastern slope or the Western Slope. Discuss the differences.

3. Draw a map of Colorado showing where the two Ute Indian reservations are today.

4. On a Colorado roadmap, find the three Western Slope counties that have only one town in them.

5. Draw a map of the Colorado River and list the towns that have grown up along it.

Books you might enjoy:

Harriet Backus. *Tomboy Bride*. Boulder: Pruett, 1969. You must read this one; none better for human interest and pure enjoyment.

George Darley. *Pioneering in the San Juan*. Lake City: Community Presbyterian Church, 1976 (reprint). A minister looks at the San Juans in the 1870s.

Robert Sloan and Carl Skowronski. *The Rainbow Route* (Mears's Silverton railroads). Denver: Sundance, 1975. Another book for railroad fans, with plenty of photographs.

Marshall Sprague. *Massacre: The Tragedy at White River*. Boston: Little, Brown, 1957. Well-written account of the Meeker Massacre.

Unit III

Unit III

	Colorado		United States
1906	Mesa Verde National Park established	1900–08	President Teddy Roosevelt preserves public lands
1913	The Big Snow	1917–18	World War I
1920	Population 939,629	1920	Population 105,710,620
1928	Moffat Tunnel opens	1929	Great Depression begins
1929	Stapleton Airport Opens	1932	President FDR begins a "New Deal" for America
1940	Population 1,123,296	1940	Population 131,669,275
1941–45	Military Bases Boom	1941–45	World War II
1950s	Auto Suburbs Boom	1956	Interstate Highway Act
1960	Population 1,753,947	1960	Population 178,464,236
1960s	"Ski Country U.S.A."	1968	First Man on the Moon
1972	Winter Olympics defeated	1973	President Nixon resigns
1970s	Oil, Coal & Solar Energy Boom	1970s	Civil Rights expanded for Women and Minority Groups
1976	Colorado's Centennial	1976	America's Bicentennial
1980	Population 2,888,834	1980	Population 226,504,825
2000	Population est. 4,000,000	2000	Population est. 260,000,000

— 12 —

Turn-of-the-Century Troubles

If you could ride a time machine back to 1900, what would you find? Many Coloradans your age would not be in school but working on farms or in factories.

You would also find many men and boys working in damp, dark mines or in hot, noisy smelters where gold and silver were taken out of ores. Miners and smelter workers often worked ten hours a day for $3 a day or less. Because of dangerous working conditions, these laborers were lucky to work a whole year without a serious accident or illness. Frequent strikes and high unemployment also made Colorado's labor scene gloomy in 1900.

Depression of 1893

People blamed many of their troubles on the federal government because it had stopped buying silver in 1893 and used only gold to back up paper money. By the end of 1893, half of Colorado's silver mines had closed, throwing about 50,000 people out of work. Hundreds of businesses failed, including many banks. Colorado, "the Silver State," sank into a depression along with the rest of the United States.

Boom days were over. One proof of this was slower population growth. Between 1870 and 1890, Colorado's population skyrocketed from 39,864 to 413,249. But between 1890 and 1900, the state grew to only 539,700. Not until 1930 would Colorado's population reach a million.

In the San Juan Mountains of southwestern Colorado, the Crash of '93 crippled the silver industry. Thirty mines closed in Rico leaving 1,200 unemployed. Ten silver mines shut down in Silverton. Nine closed in Telluride. Twenty closed in Ouray. As the supply of silver ore fell, silver smelters closed.

Henry Strater, founder of Durango's famous Strater Hotel, lowered his room and meal rates. Still he could not attract enough business to cover his debts and had to sell his grand hotel. Another Durangoan, thirty-six-year-old Frank Burke, blew off the top of his head with a shotgun. He left behind a note:

> Good bye all friends. Times too hard.
> The Boys can have a wake . . . What I owe now I'll owe forever.

Onetime mining millionaires went into debt and had to sell everything. Horace Tabor, best known of the silver kings, was forced to sell his mines, opera houses and office buildings. He even had to sell his mansion on Capitol Hill in Denver. The Tabors and their two little girls moved into the Windsor Hotel on Larimer Street. The second Mrs. Tabor, a beauty known as "Baby Doe," once wore a $7,000 wedding dress and a $75,000 diamond necklace, but spent her last years wearing rags and using gunny sacks for shoes. She survived until 1935, when her frozen body was found in a shack at the Matchless Mine in Leadville.

The nationwide depression of 1893 hurt farmers and ranchers as well as miners. Agriculture was in trouble because of drought, overgrazing, and soil erosion. The Crash of '93 made it hard for farmers and ranchers to pay their debts or to get new loans from banks. Many people lost their land because they could not make mortgage payments.

In 1894, hundreds of these homeless, jobless people drifted into Denver. The city let them camp along the South Platte River and tried to feed them. As the army of unemployed grew to over 1,000, Denver officials worried about disease, crime, and riots. City leaders told the jobless to take their problems to the federal government. Coloradans and other unemployed Americans planned a protest march to Washington, D.C. When

some of them finally reached the national capitol, their leaders were arrested for walking on the government's grass. The defeated protestors went back to their homes—if they had homes to go to—as hungry and poor as ever.

The Populist Party

The Depression of 1893 led to political unrest. Many felt that neither the Democrats nor the Republicans could deal with the country's problems. So they turned to a new political party called the People's Party or the Populists. The Populists, who organized on a national level in 1891, talked about reforming the political system and doing more for farmers, miners, and factory workers. This new political party hoped to:

(1) Have the federal government buy up all the silver that could be produced at $1.28 an ounce and use it to make more money.

(2) Nationalize (have the government own and operate) the railroads and lower freight rates.

(3) Set up a maximum work day of eight hours.

(4) Start taxing people's income instead of their landholdings, and have richer people pay a larger share of the taxes.

Hundreds of unemployed Coloradans drifted into Denver after 1893. Many of them were housed in this relief camp along the South Platte River. If you had been in their boots, what would you have done?
—Denver Public Library

(5) Let voters draw up and circulate petitions to change laws or make new ones.

(6) Use the secret ballot in elections.

Many Americans liked these ideas. In 1892 Coloradans elected the Populist candidate for governor, Davis H. Waite. Governor Waite, a newspaper editor from Aspen, was an old man with a long beard and a loud voice. He promised to reform Colorado even if "blood should flow to our horses' bridles." After he said this, the governor's enemies called him "Bloody Bridles" Waite. One of his reforms almost did cause bloodshed during the City Hall War.

The City Hall War

Like many Coloradans to this day, Governor Waite felt that Denver was a wicked place. Proof of the city's corruption had come in 1891 when Denver Mayor Wolfe Londoner was forced to resign. A court trial showed that he had been elected with hundreds of illegal votes.

When he was elected, Governor Waite complained that some of the saloons and gambling halls in Denver never closed, and fired two police commissioners for letting these places stay open despite the law. The two fired Denver officials said they would rather fight than leave their jobs. Governor Waite called out the state militia, which surrounded City Hall with Gatling guns and cannons. Policemen and firemen who worked for the commissioners went down to City Hall to prevent the governor and his troops from kicking out their bosses. Soon the windows of Denver's City Hall bristled with rifles and pistols.

According to one story, the gambler "Soapy" Smith climbed to the top of the City Hall bell tower and began waving a stick of dynamite. "I'm closer to heaven than you gentlemen," Soapy yelled down at the governor's soldiers. "But if you come any closer, you may get there first!" A huge crowd gathered to see the battle. Governor Waite, however, avoided bloodshed by withdrawing his troops. (The site is marked today by the old City Hall bell at Fourteenth and Larimer Streets near Larimer Square.) Denver remained unreformed. Efforts to reform Cripple Creek, Leadville, Pueblo, and other Colorado cities also failed.

Women

Governor Waite and the Populists were more successful in their plan to let women vote. As we have seen, Colorado women were first allowed to register and vote in 1894. Many women entered politics at this time because new goods and machines helped free them from housework. New inventions like electric iceboxes, sewing machines, vacuum cleaners, and other appliances made it easier to manage a household. Factory-made clothing and packaged food enabled women to spend less time sewing and cooking. Even before these advances, women had worked in fields, factories, and businesses as well as in the home. During the 1880s, over 800 "Cattle Queens" ran ranches in Colorado. One of the most famous cattlewomen was Elizabeth Iliff. After the death of her husband, John W. Iliff, Elizabeth took over their vast cattle kingdom and ran it in a very able way. Other nineteenth-century women added to their family's income by taking in boarders, baby-sitting, and running shops, restaurants, hotels, and other businesses. Farm women often sold butter and eggs, poultry and produce. With advanced technology, women could handle not only home-based businesses but could also move out into the labor force.

Once they could vote, women began making even bigger contributions. They worked for better schools, churches, and health care. Women's clubs fought everything from political corruption to promiscuous expectoration (spitting). Individual women ran newspapers like Sarah Churchill's *Queen Bee*, a Denver weekly. Women also wrote many best-selling books, such as Helen Hunt Jackson's *A Century of Dishonor*, which drew national attention to the mistreatment of American Indians. Mary Lathrop, a Denver resident, became the state's first female attorney. Her services were sought by some of the most notorious men in Colorado, including Denver's leading gambler, "Big Ed" Chase. In the 1894 election, three women were elected to the state legislature. Some talked of the day when Colorado would have a female governor and senator.

Governor Davis H. Waite, an Aspen newspaper editor, tried to reform Colorado government. His efforts to help miners, farmers and blue collar workers were usually defeated by the state legislature.
—Tom Noel Collection

DID YOU KNOW:

- That there were twenty males for each female in Colorado in 1860. By 1900, there were five women for every six men.
- That Colorado has had 100 different railroads over the years. Many of them went out of business after the Crash of 1893.
- That Denver had almost 500 different grocery stores in 1900.
- That German-born people were the most numerous ethnic group in Colorado in 1900.
- That Illinois-born people were the most numerous American-born immigrants to Colorado in 1900.

Many of Colorado's strikes were settled by the Colorado National Guard. The Guard protected mine owners, their mines and "scab" labor from strikers. Why is this fort-like fence and guard posted at the Emmett Mine in Leadville during the 1896 strike?
—Amon Carter Museum

Labor Unions

As we have seen, the Cripple Creek gold boom of the 1890s was one of the few bright spots in Colorado after the 1893 crash. Miners and mine owners of Cripple Creek had agreed in 1894 that miners would work no more than eight hours a day for no less than $3 a day.

The miners' biggest union was the Western Federation of Miners (WFM). This union, headquartered in Denver, tried to organize hard rock miners throughout the West. By 1903, the WFM had forty-two locals in Colorado. The union's star promoter was William D. Haywood, nicknamed "Big Bill." He stood nearly six feet tall, weighed over 225 pounds and had only one good eye.

Big Bill started working in the mines when he was a teenager. It was dangerous work. He saw a rock fall from the roof of the mine and crush a friend's head. Shortly afterwards, Big Bill smashed his own hand in a mine mishap. While he was unable to work, his family went hungry because there was no workmen's insurance or compensation in those days. These accidents and the working conditions in most mines convinced Haywood that working people should unionize for safer, more rewarding work.

Despite the 1894 Cripple Creek agreement, many Coloradans still labored ten or even twelve hours a day for low wages. In 1903, Haywood and the WFM began a statewide crusade for the $3, eight-hour day. From Idaho Springs to Cripple Creek, from Leadville to Telluride, miners walked off the job. Numerous brawls, injuries, and several murders created bitterness between labor and management. Violence peaked on June 6, 1904, when someone dynamited the Independence Mine depot in the Cripple Creek District, killing thirteen men and injuring many more.

Whereas Governor Waite had sided with the miners in 1894, Governor James H. Peabody sided with the mine owners after his election in 1902. Governor Peabody sent in the Colorado National Guard to protect the mines and strikebreakers. Striking miners were illegally arrested, locked in "bull pens," and even loaded on railroad cars and shipped to Kansas. The *New York Times* for August 11, 1904, called Colorado's 1903–1904 labor wars "a reign of terror." The strikers were crushed and so was their union, the WFM.

WILLIAM D. HAYWOOD
Secretary-Treasurer Western Federation of Miners

"Big Bill" Haywood tried to unionize Colorado miners to fight for a minimum wage of three dollars a day and a maximum work day of eight hours.
—Denver Public Library

Three Governors In One Day

Although Governor Peabody defeated the Western Federation of Miners, he made enemies in doing so. In the 1904 election, Coloradans voted him out of office. However, the Republican-controlled supreme court and state legislature charged that the Democratic winner, Alva B. Adams, had been elected with illegal votes. They reinstated Peabody. Angry Democrats then persuaded the Republicans to replace Peabody with his Lieutenant Governor, Jesse F. McDonald of Leadville. This farce of three governors in one day suggested that Colorado had reached an all-time low in political confusion and corruption.

Some Coloradans were shocked by the rotten politics, miserable working conditions, and poverty of the working class at the turn of the century. A few determined men and women decided that the time had come to begin a social, political, and economic reform of Colorado.

QUESTIONS:

1. What would a weekday be like for a person your age in 1900?
2. What kind of work were most Coloradans doing in 1900?
3. What federal action ended Colorado's silver boom? Why?
4. Do you agree with the Populist party ideas? How many of their plans have become law today?
5. What are some reasons why Davis H. Waite was Colorado's most controversial governor?
6. Has there been a change in the role of women since 1900?
7. What were Colorado miners striking for in 1903–04?

ACTIVITIES:

1. Visit a nursing home and ask some of the people there what life was like when they were your age. What do your grandparents and the elderly people in your neighborhood say about this? Do they remember "the good old days" or "the bad old days"?

2. To find out what school was like around 1900, you can visit the Colorado Heritage Center in Denver. Ask to see the old Broadway School classroom.

3. To find out what mining was like, you can tour mines in Central City, Cripple Creek, Georgetown, Leadville, and other mining towns. See if you would like to be a miner.

4. In your school library (or the public library), look up your town's newspaper for March 17, 1905 (and the day afterward). What does it say about the day Colorado had three governors?

Books you might enjoy:

The Colorado Chronicles. Volume 2: Famous Colorado Women. Frederick, Colorado: Jende-Hagan Bookcorp, 1981.

Edwina Fallis. *When Denver and I Were Young.* Denver: Big Mountain Press, 1956.

Stewart H. Holbrook. *The Rocky Mountain Revolution.* New York: Henry Holt & Co., 1956. Readable account of Harry Orchard and the industrial warfare that ripped Colorado apart in the first two decades of the twentieth century.

Terry William Mangan. *Colorado on Glass: Colorado's First Half-Century as Seen by the Camera.* Denver: Sundance, 1975. A superb pictorial review.

Representative Men of Colorado. Denver: Rowell, 1902.

Representative Women of Colorado. Denver: Williamson-Haffner, 1911. If you can find these rare books or other illustrated history books published around 1900, take a peek at the hair styles and costumes to see how Coloradans looked then.

George C. Suggs. *Colorado's War on Militant Unionism.* Detroit: Wayne State Univ. Press, 1972.

James E. Wright. *The Politics of Populism: Dissent in Colorado.* New Haven: Yale Univ. Press, 1974.

13

Reformers

Benjamin Barr Lindsey was a tiny man. He weighed ninety-eight pounds and stood barely five feet, five inches tall, but he stands tallest among Colorado's reformers. Lindsey spent his life working for the poor and the powerless and especially for their children.

Perhaps Lindsey loved underdogs because he grew up as one. His family came to Denver in 1880, from a farm in Tennessee, when Ben was ten. They moved into a shack on West Colfax Avenue. After Ben's father committed suicide, the boy began delivering the *Rocky Mountain News* in the morning and working as a janitor at night. He also kept going to school and did not stop until he became a lawyer.

Constant hard work and poverty depressed Ben, as he recalled later in his book, *The Beast*:

> It seemed to me that my life was not worth living—that every one had lost faith in me—that I should never succeed in the law or anything else—that I had no brains—that I should never do anything but scrub floors and run messages . . . . I got a revolver and some cartridges, locked myself in my room, confronted myself desperately in the mirror, put the muzzle of the loaded pistol to my temple, and pulled the trigger.

The gun misfired and Lindsey took a second look at his life. He decided "to crush the circumstances that had almost crushed me." Thus began Ben Lindsey's lifelong crusade to help humanity.

Judge Ben Lindsey (with moustache at far left) was not much bigger than many of the Juvenile Delinquents he worked with on the Juvenile Court. Why was the "Kid's Judge" so popular?
—Colorado Historical Society

His first priority was the treatment of juvenile delinquents. Lindsey found that putting young offenders in jail with older criminals was like sending them to a school for crime. Adults in prison would tell youngsters how to steal, use weapons, and commit other crimes. After Lindsey became a judge, he created separate courts and separate prisons for people aged sixteen or younger. The "Kids' Judge" made the Denver Juvenile Court a model not only for America, but for the world. In a 1914 national poll for *American Magazine*, the Denver judge was listed among the ten "greatest living Americans."

The little judge had many big ideas for reform. Among other things, he attacked child labor, divorce laws, corrupt politics, and powerful corporations he felt had too much political influence. But Lindsey soon found that neither the Democrats nor the Republicans would help him, so he ran as an independent candidate for Governor of Colorado in 1906. Later, Lindsey and other Coloradans joined former president Theodore Roosevelt in forming a new party, the Progressives. Lindsey made many enemies, including the Ku Klux Klan. During the 1920s he left Colorado for California, where he kept crusading for reform until his death in 1943.

Governor Shafroth

Another man who worked hard for reform in Colorado was John F. Shafroth. He became a favorite of reformers in 1904 when he resigned from the U.S. House of Representatives. Shafroth refused to continue in office, saying that some people had voted for him illegally. Voters remembered that in 1908 and elected "Honest John" governor. He held that post until 1913 when he was elected to the U.S. Senate.

As governor, Shafroth helped turn some of the ideas of Governor Waite and the Populists into law. For example, Colorado adopted the voter initiative process in 1910, after voters approved this tool of democratic government. The initiative means that if you think a law should be passed you can draw up a petition. If enough people sign your petition, the issue goes on the ballot at election time so that everyone can vote on your idea. Thus the people, as well as the governor and the legislature, can now make laws.

Many other reforms took place during the Shafroth administration. Campaign contributions from corporations were regulated. Voters were given a chance to help pick their party's candidates in primary elections. A Public Utilities Commission was set up to serve as a watchdog over agencies providing electricity, gas, water, transportation, and other utilities. Earlier, in 1907, a state civil service law was passed to stop the "spoils system," under which a governor could fire state employees at will.

An eight-hour workday law was passed for mining and other dangerous occupations. State inspectors started to go down into mines and out into factories to look for work hazards and to report abuses of the new child labor laws. Still, passing laws and reporting violations of them was not always the solution. Sometimes they were not or could not be enforced.

For example, one of the deadliest labor wars in American history occurred in spite of new labor laws after Colorado coal miners went on strike in 1913. Their union, the United Mine Workers, wanted a wage increase, stricter enforcement of the eight-hour workday law, safer working conditions, and the right to live outside company towns.

The Colorado Fuel and Iron Company, which controlled many Colorado coal mines, refused to recognize the United Mine Workers and their demands. Thus began a bitter, bloody strike which led to the Ludlow Massacre of April 1914. Strikers and their families, after being thrown out of the company towns, moved into tents at Ludlow, a railroad siding between Walsenburg and Trinidad. There they were surrounded by the Colorado National Guard armed with machine guns. To escape the gunfire, strikers and their families dug holes to hide in under their tents.

After this tent town caught fire on April 20, 1914, two women and eleven children were found suffocated in their foxholes. Although the United Mine Workers lost lives and the strike, they erected a large monument at Ludlow to remind people of the struggle.

Governor Shafroth was also interested in prison reform. He put Thomas J. Tynan in charge of the state penitentiary at Canon City. Tynan found that some 700 inmates just sat around twiddling their thumbs. He said this "sort of got on my nerves" and put the convicts to work building roads, running a ranch, growing their own food, and building a new prison hospital. Because of Tynan's programs, the penitentiary in Canon City became a busier, less troubled place. Taxpayers, of course, were delighted that these work projects cut the cost of running the prison.

Josephine Roche

Josephine Roche, the daughter of a mine owner, worked with Judge Lindsey to make Colorado a better place to bring up children and later on her own she tried to improve working conditions for miners. She became Denver's first policewoman in 1913. Officer Roche, according to Judge Lindsey, "could break up a dance hall row or a riot in front of a saloon better than an experienced policeman." Known as Denver's "lady cop," she visited dance halls at night to enforce a city law that required anyone under twenty-one to write down his or her name and address. If you did not sign in, you were not allowed into the dance.

When Josephine's father died in 1927, she became the biggest stockholder of the Rocky Mountain Fuel Company. Now she was able to tackle an issue that had troubled her for years. At the age of twelve, she had asked her father if he would show her one of his coal mines.

"It would be too dangerous," he told her.

"Then how is it safe for the miners?" the little girl asked. Her father did not have an answer.

After Josephine grew up and inherited stock in the coal company, she visited its six mines. She found out just how unsafe they were and took steps to improve them. In 1928, she raised the base wage to $7 a day, the highest salary paid in the Colorado mining industry. Other mine owners criticized her and predicted that the Rocky Mountain Fuel Company would lose money and soon fail.

When the Great Depression of 1929 brought hard times, Josephine donated her salary as vice president to help keep the Rocky Mountain Fuel Company open. The United Mine Workers union loaned money to the company so it could continue business while many other mines were closing. Because Josephine had worked with the union instead of against it, the miners also volunteered to accept wage cuts and work fewer days so that no one would have to be laid off.

This happy solution to Great Depression problems attracted the interest of President Franklin D. Roosevelt and his wife, Eleanor. They asked Josephine to come to Washington and become Assistant Secretary of the Treasury. She accepted and became the second most important woman in the federal government (the first was Frances Perkins, the Secretary of Labor, who had been Josephine's classmate at Columbia University). Josephine later served as director of the National Youth Administration and the Public Health Service.

In 1934, Josephine Roche added another first to her long list by becoming the first woman to run for governor of Colorado. She narrowly lost the Democratic Party nomination to Edwin C. Johnson, a farmer from Craig.

Emily Griffith

Another woman who worked for reform was Emily Griffith, a Denver school teacher. She saw that many Coloradans were handicapped by a lack of work skills and by not being able to speak, read, and write English well. In 1916, she opened her Opportunity School. It offered free courses in hundreds of different subjects "for all who wished to learn." Evening and weekend courses were held for working people. Today, the Emily Griffith Opportunity School still teaches students of all ages how to fix everything from automobiles to airplanes, to run computers and word processors, and hundreds of other skills that help them find jobs.

Boss Speer

While some men and women tried to improve jobs, jails and schools, others began to look closely at the Colorado landscape and its cities. They found that the state needed a face lift. The best known of Colorado's city beautifiers was Mayor Robert W. Speer of Denver. He came to Colorado from Pennsylvania with raw and bleeding lungs. He and thousands of other tuberculosis (T.B.) victims had been told by their doctors to try the high, dry Colorado climate. These "lungers" flooded into the state, creating a health rush as big as the mining rushes. T.B. hospitals were built all over the state. On the streets you would see people coughing into sputum cups. Nowadays, new drugs and better health care have almost wiped out T.B., but it used to be the nation's number one killer.

Speer, like many other lung disease victims, thrived on the

sunshine and low humidity, and once his health began to improve, he jumped into politics. He and others persuaded the state legislature to create the City and County of Denver. Denver, which had 133,859 citizens in 1900, had been part of Arapahoe County. It needed a stronger government to cope with its special problems. After the new county was created, Littleton replaced Denver as the county seat of Arapahoe County.

With the help of many illegal votes, Speer was elected mayor of the new City and County of Denver in 1904. He was called a "boss" because of his powerful and corrupt political machine. "I am a boss," Speer admitted, but added, "I want to be a good one." He was.

One of "Boss" Speer's first orders was to remove the "Keep Off the Grass" signs from city parks. Then he converted the

Although Mayor Robert W. Speer had no children, he made Denver a better place for kids. He built playgrounds, ball fields and swimming pools.
—Amon Carter Museum

banks of Cherry Creek, which had been used as a dump, to Speer Boulevard. The new mayor also began buying land to create more parks. Parkways were built between the parks so that you could walk, run, or bicycle all over town on paths edged with trees, shrubs, and flowers. Coloradans found plenty to do when they visited Denver parks; Mayor Speer put in playgrounds, tennis courts, and golf courses and built lakes for fishing, swimming, boating, and ice skating in winter.

Speer also installed miles of sewers, paved streets, and sandstone sidewalks. Fancy street lights and trash cans were put on downtown streets, and he tried to outlaw billboards, bury power lines, and limit building heights to save Denver's view of the mountains. When Speer died in office in 1918, he had given away 116,000 shade trees, doubled the park space, and improved public health, education, and welfare. Denver became one of the handsomest big cities in the United States.

John Otto

Other Coloradans began to be concerned with caring for the natural environment. In Mesa County, a man named John Otto settled near Grand Junction among some fabulous red-stone canyons carved by the Colorado River. In May of 1907 he wrote:

> I came here last year and found these canyons, and they feel like the heart of the world to me. I'm going to stay and build trails and promote this place, because it should be a national park. Some folks think I'm crazy, but I want to see this scenery opened up to all people . . . .

Otto worked and fought until the Colorado National Monument was created on the outskirts of Grand Junction in 1911. Otto became the area's caretaker at a salary of $1 a month. Although Otto got his monument, he lost his wife. She left him in 1911, explaining in a letter to her parents that she "could not live with a man to whom even a cabin was an encumbrance. He wanted to live in tents or without tents, outdoors."

She left for good but he stayed with the Colorado National Monument, always working to improve and promote it. Today thousands of tourists admire the spectacular canyons and enjoy the views of nearby Grand Mesa and the Book Cliffs, which look like partly opened books.

Enos Mills

Colorado's best-known naturalist was Enos Mills. At the age of fourteen, Mills left the Kansas flatlands for the mountains of Colorado. Arriving in Estes Park, he found a job at the Elkhorn Lodge washing dishes, chopping wood, and serving afternoon tea to the tourists.

Enos Mills, father of Rocky Mountain National Park, pointed out that the Rockies were both a winter and summer playground.
—Denver Public Library

During his spare time, Enos explored the mountains. He learned to love the alpine meadows, the spruce and aspen forests, and the flower-lined mountain brooks. He wanted to share them with others and began guiding tourists into the back country. To be nearer to his beloved mountains, Mills built a log cabin (now a museum) at the base of Longs Peak.

Mills spent winters as well as summers in the mountains in order to enjoy the "frozen music" of the snowbound Rockies. He camped out alone under the stars or in snow caves, skied the Continental Divide and raced avalanches. He tracked grizzly bears, watched beavers build their homes, and studied the rocks that showed how glaciers had carved out mountain valleys.

Mills began writing magazine articles and books that were read all over America. Soon people asked him to give talks on the Rockies. In his writings and his speeches, this self-educated naturalist crusaded for preservation of at least one small section of the Rockies. He wanted a national park. The Colorado Mountain Club, still a big and important group of mountain lovers, also fought for a park. They claimed that a mountain park would be a place where everyone could enjoy hiking, fishing, picnicking, camping, skiing, and snowshoeing—or just watching the marmots and mule deer, the elk, and the water ouzels.

In 1915, the dream of Enos Mills and others came true when President Woodrow Wilson signed a bill in Washington, creating Rocky Mountain National Park.

Because Enos Mills was a radical conservationist with little tolerance for anyone who opposed him, he made many enemies. Cattle and sheep raisers, miners and timbermen who had used the land resented him and his ideas about conservation. Other critics thought that state and local governments, not federal agencies, should control Colorado land use.

Some people must have been relieved when Enos Mills died in 1922, but his friend Judge Ben Lindsey declared that:

> Like all great men, Enos Mills was perhaps least appreciated while he lived. . . . I think all will agree that Mills, his work and what he stood for, cannot be too much known and understood. It means far more to our children than the work of men after whom many of our mountain peaks have been named. Some of these men, like Zebulon Pike, discovered the bodies of our mountains. Mills discovered their souls.

Particularly as twentieth-century life becomes more crowded and urban, Coloradans have grown to appreciate people like Enos Mills and John Otto who fought for national monuments, parks, forests, and grasslands. Can you imagine what our state would be like without any public parks?

The two decades between the Spanish American War of 1898 and America's involvement in World War I in 1917 are known as the Progressive Era. Thanks to these dedicated people and many others, there was certainly progress in Colorado.

DID YOU KNOW:

- That Arapaho Indians named the Never Summer Mountains in Rocky Mountain National Park. Their word was *Ni-chebe-chii*, which actually translates as Never-No-Summer.
- That there are only two Indian reservations left in Colorado.
- That you can find ripples from ancient inland oceans in the sandstone of the Colorado National Monument.
- That Denver's mountain parks include a ski area, Winter Park.
- That Denver has the world's most famous Juvenile Court.

QUESTIONS:

1. Teenage crime is one of the growing problems in America. What did Judge Ben Lindsey think should be done about it?
2. Why was Josephine Roche able to pay her miners better and still keep her mines open when others were closing?
3. List some of the accomplishments of Josephine Roche.
4. Why do adults often go to schools like the Emily Griffith Opportunity School for continuing education classes?
5. When were the parks nearest your home created?
6. Why did the naturalist Enos Mills make enemies?
7. What types of reforms were successful in Colorado during the Progressive reform era?

ACTIVITIES:

1. Sit in on a juvenile court case in your town. How are young lawbreakers treated differently from adult criminals today?

2. Do the parks, playgrounds, and waterways in your community need beautification? Organize a cleanup and keep a list of all the different litter you find. One person's trash may be another person's treasure! Look for old coins, tokens, and bottles. How much can you get for bottles, cans, and newspapers that you recycle?

3. How many of Colorado's national parks, monuments, forests and grasslands have you visited? Ask other members of the class to discuss the ones they have visited.

4. What recreational and educational programs do your local, state, and national parks offer for your class? (Just look them up in the phone book and call to ask.)

Books you might enjoy:

Sonora Babb. *An Owl on Every Post*. New York: McCall, 1970. Beautifully written memoirs of a young girl who lived in a sod house in 1913 on a farm in southeastern Colorado.

Elinor Bluemel. *The Opportunity School and Emily Griffith, Its Founder*. Denver: Green Mountain Press, 1970.

Marjorie Hornbein. "Josephine Roche: Social Worker and Coal Operator." *Colorado Magazine*, 53 (Summer, 1976), pp. 243–260.

Ben B. Lindsey and Harvey J. O'Higgins. *The Beast*. New York: Doubleday, Page & Co., 1910.

Enos A. Mills. *The Spell of the Rockies*. Boston: Houghton Mifflin, 1911.

Colorado Fever is a generously illustrated, highly readable magazine published bi-monthly by the Colorado Historical Institute for Children, Inc., 2710 East Exposition Avenue, Denver, Colorado 80209. It is produced by and available from Jende-Hagen Bookcorp., Frederick, Colorado.

—14—

Twentieth-Century Changes

Many of the major trends of our century began in the 1920s. During that decade, life was greatly speeded up in Colorado and all over the U.S. by the introduction of two new transportation systems—the automobile and the airplane—and by new electronic technology such as the radio. During the 1920s many people also began to move out of small city homes and apartments into suburban neighborhoods with bigger houses and yards.

All of these changes cost money, but the 1920s were a relatively prosperous time. World War I had played a part in strengthening the economy. When this war began in Europe in 1914, Colorado farmers and ranchers found European markets for their crops and livestock, and Colorado's mining industry enjoyed new booms in copper, lead, zinc, tungsten, molybdenum, and coal.

World War I, of course, was also a tragic time. About 43,000 Coloradans joined the armed services and 1,000 of these gave their lives for our country. After the war ended on November 11, 1918, an even deadlier menace swept the globe—the 1918–19 worldwide flu epidemic, which killed over 500,000 Americans. Every community in Colorado mourned its losses.

Following the double tragedy of war and flu, the 1920s proved to be a safer, happier decade. Colorado developed a

Before automobile bridges were built across the Colorado at Grand Junction, this was the way you got across.
—The Museum of Western Colorado

diversified economic base that included mining, agriculture, industry, commerce, and tourism. Most Coloradans received decent wages for a forty-hour work week, and many families saved money to buy their own homes in new suburbs.

Water

These new suburbs were made possible by another twentieth century trend in Colorado—massive water projects. In the old days, people usually settled along creeks or rivers or where there was well water. But in the early decades of the twentieth century, the federal, state, and local governments began building dams and tunnels to deliver water to wherever people wanted to live.

Water projects continue to be a key to Colorado's growth today, although they are growing more controversial and more costly to build. In Colorado, these projects have often taken water from the sparsely populated mountains, where most of the precipitation falls, to the much more heavily populated, but more arid eastern slope. Western Slopers have resented losing this water which is so important to their towns, mines, ranches, and fruit orchards. Yet it was Western Slopers who benefited from the first major rearrangement of Colorado's waterways. This U.S. Reclamation Service project of 1910 funneled Gunnison River water through a tunnel under Vernal Mesa to the farms and ranches around Delta and Montrose.

A few years later, Roaring Fork water was diverted, piped underneath Independence Pass to Twin Lakes, and then put into the Arkansas River to benefit sugar beet and melon growers downstream. More recently, the Fryingpan-Arkansas project has taken more water from the Aspen area for the Arkansas River, which waters Leadville, Salida, Canon City, Pueblo, La Junta, Las Animas, Lamar, and many smaller towns.

The Colorado River, with headwaters in Rocky Mountain National Park, was dammed by the Big Thompson-Colorado Project, creating Lake Granby and Shadow Mountain Reservoir in the 1940s. Water from these man-made lakes was then channeled back under the Continental Divide in a thirteen-mile tunnel that empties at Estes Park into the Big Thompson River. Since hydroelectric plants were a part of this $169 million project, electricity as well as water was provided for northeastern Colorado.

The City of Denver, located on the east side of the Rocky Mountains, taps water sources on the western slopes of the Rockies, and pipes a good portion of its supply to residents of the Metropolitan Area through tunnels under the Continental Divide.

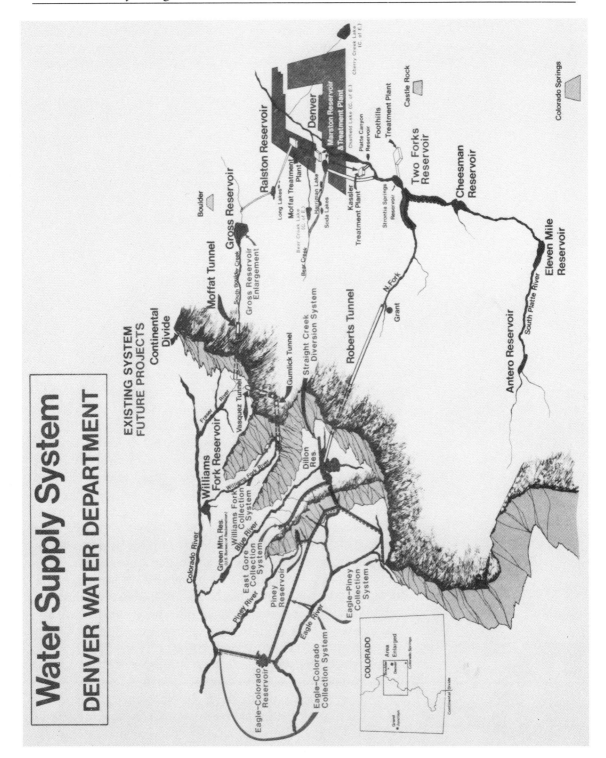

Water Supply System

DENVER WATER DEPARTMENT

EXISTING SYSTEM
FUTURE PROJECTS

Stream diversions, irrigation ditches, deep wells, and motorized equipment enabled agriculture to flower on the plains during the first twenty years of the twentieth century. Sugar beets and Russian wheat became as important as mining had been to Colorado's economy. Agriculture, like mining, had its ups and downs, its booms and busts. After the good years from 1900 to 1920, lower farm prices, the Crash of 1929, and the "Black Blizzards" of the 1930s Dust Bowl era left the eastern plains littered with ghost towns. Dry ditches, broken windmills, and the sunbaked skeletons of abandoned farmhouses are a reminder that farming can be as risky as mining in Colorado, where only a dozen inches of rain may fall in a year.

New Industries, New Technology

Water was not the only drink to interest Coloradans during the 1920s. In a statewide vote, a majority decided to outlaw alcohol beginning January 1, 1916. But many people voted against prohibition, and some of them continued to drink regardless of the law. Leadville and other depressed mining towns discovered a new industry—making moonshine whiskey. Old mines proved to be perfect hideouts for stills. Whole trainloads of beet sugar traveled to Leadville and became "Leadville Moon," the most famous of many Colorado bootleg brands. To deliver the moonshine, autos were customized with big engines up front and big, secret trunks and heavy load suspension in the rear.

Another liquid that became precious during the twentieth century was oil. Colorado's first oil well had been dug near Florence in 1862, but the oil industry did not begin to boom until the 1920s, when the auto age began to accelerate.

Electric radio sets and record players also became popular during that decade. New dance crazes like the Charleston swept the country, to the distress of parents, and young "swingers" danced late into the night to electronic music. The switch from silent movies to "talkies" added to the noise level.

The telephone, which had been around since the 1880s, became a common sight in homes. "Ma Bell," as Mountain States Telephone Company has been nicknamed, was formed in 1911 as a combination of various smaller, competing phone companies. Today US West (successor to Mountain Bell) is one of Colorado's biggest employers and nearly every household has at least one telephone.

The radio, or "wireless," was introduced to Colorado in 1920 by Dr. W.D. Reynolds, a Colorado Springs physician, who founded KLZ, the first radio station in Colorado. In 1924 the powerful KOA station began broadcasting from Denver, and by 1950 Colorado had thirty-four radio broadcasting stations. In 1952, the first television station, Channel 2, began operations in Denver. Channel 6, the pioneer public broadcasting and educational station, first went on the air in 1956.

Before automobiles invaded Colorado, bicycles were popular. The fad began back in 1879 when a Denver shopkeeper began selling Columbia bicycles. Few people bought these early "bone shakers," so the bicycle salesman rented out a dance hall and offered riding lessons. He also tried to promote two-wheelers by bicycling around the city, but the police arrested him for scaring horses.

Only after the arrival of air tires, good brakes, and ball-bearing wheels did bicycling become popular. By 1900, the Denver Wheel Club boasted 25,000 members. Bicycle clubs across the state competed in century rides—pedaling 100 miles in 12 hours or less.

One magazine claimed that "for the cyclist, exhaltation and exhilaration take the place of depression and weakness," and added that the exercise would bring a sparkle to your eye, pink to your cheeks and brush away "cobwebs in the brain."

Bicyclists, after fighting potholes, mud and dust, organized to pressure city councils, county commissioners and the state legislature to build better roads. These improved highways paved the way for automobiles that drove many two-wheelers off the road. By the 1920s, the automobile craze replaced the bicycle craze. Bicycles did not make a major comeback until the 1970s.

Age of the Auto

The fast-growing popularity of automobiles in the early part of this century eventually doomed the old streetcar systems. Once Aspen, Boulder, Colorado Springs, Cripple Creek, Denver, Durango, Fort Collins, Grand Junction, Greeley, Pueblo, and Trinidad all had streetcars. Horses pulled the first streetcars; until they were replaced by electric trolleys. Streetcars enabled cities to grow outward into streetcar suburbs—neighborhoods along or near streetcar lines. Many of these early suburbs were later annexed to the mother city. Other suburbs, such as Aurora, Englewood, Littleton, and Lakewood in the Denver area, have remained independent towns. Although suburbanization began with streetcars, automobiles have greatly speeded up the process.

One of the first cars in Colorado was ordered by David W. Brunton, a Denver mining engineer. It was shipped to Denver from Boston in pieces. Brunton spent a whole day putting his electric car together, and on May 10, 1899, took it for a spin on the streets of Denver. Crowds followed the "horseless carriage" around to see how it would behave.

Automobile ads began appearing in the newspapers, such as this one in the *Denver Post* on May 1, 1900:

> $750   LOCOMOBILE $750
> The famous Steam Wagon. Cheap to buy.
> Cheap to run. No noise, odor, or vibration.
> Any person can run it from one to 40 miles per hour.

Dr. F.L. Bartlett of Canon City ordered an Oldsmobile in 1901. After finally putting together all the pieces shipped from Detroit, the doctor went to a nearby pasture to practice starting, stopping, and steering. Then Canon City's main street was cleared of all horses so he could try out the first internal combustion car in Colorado. Dr. Bartlett gave free rides to anyone brave enough to climb into his machine.

With the increasing demand for better roads, the Colorado State Highway Commission was created in 1909. After the Federal Highway Act passed in 1916, Colorado received federal matching funds for road construction. By 1921 our state was spending over $10 million a year to build auto routes.

Spencer Penrose

Towns began to measure their progress in miles of paved roads. Some farsighted people realized that automobiles would turn Colorado into a tourist haven. One of them was Spencer Penrose, who had made a fortune in Cripple Creek gold and retired to Colorado Springs. Penrose tried out a new car every year, spending as much as $5,000 per vehicle. With a stable full of horseless carriages, Penrose had a vested interest in the good roads campaign. To prove that automobiles could master the mountains, Penrose built an auto road to the top of Pike's Peak.

As America's best known mountain, Pike's Peak had long attracted tourists to Colorado Springs, but the new road brought car caravans. To entertain his fellow automobile lovers, Penrose started the Pike's Peak Hill Climb on July 4, 1916. This demanding race still attracts daredevil drivers who roar up the 14,110-foot mountain faster than a mile a minute.

After Penrose found that people came from all over the world for the race, he turned the old Broadmoor Hotel into a $2 million resort. To this day the Broadmoor is the most famous resort hotel in Colorado.

This automobile smashed up next to the State Capitol in Denver. Can you see why drivers fought for better roads?
—Denver Water Board/ Tom Noel Collection

Automobile Tourists

Automobiles allowed both residents and out-of-state visitors to tour Colorado in ever-increasing numbers. Soon tourism became a major part of Colorado's economy. Exploring ghost towns became a popular pastime after a woman from Boulder began prowling old mining towns in the 1920s. She was Muriel Sibell Wolle, an art professor at the University of Colorado at Boulder. Although rough auto trips into remote and rugged mountain ghost towns terrified her, Wolle managed to visit nearly every ghost town in Colorado. Once she reached a town, she talked to old residents about it, read its newspapers, and drew sketches of the decaying buildings and mines. She put all this together in *Stampede to Timberline*, a ghost town guidebook popular since its first appearance in 1949.

Automobile tourists also delighted in Colorado's many natural hot springs. Eldorado Springs, Glenwood Springs, Idaho Springs, Ouray, Manitou Springs, and Steamboat Springs were among the most famous. To make automobile touring inexpensive, many towns set up auto camps where motorists could put up tents. The auto campers of the 1920s were the descendants of the prairie schooner pioneers and forerunners of the camper and mobile home travelers common in Colorado today.

Boulder's Chautauqua Park, Canon City's Royal Gorge, Denver's Elitch Gardens, the Italian Cave in Julesburg, Pueblo's Mineral Palace, and Wray's Flirtation Point lured vacationers. Yet the Rockies remained the greatest attraction, a place to cool off with a snowball fight even in August.

Airplanes

Not long after automobiles appeared, people began experimenting with wings and car engines. The auto age soon became the air age. Various Coloradans had been tinkering with airplanes for a decade before Denver built a municipal airport. What began as two dusty runways, a tiny terminal, and a windsock is now Stapleton International Airport.

Originally, pilots avoided Colorado for the same reason that the first railroads did—the mountains were too high, too dangerous, and too expensive to cross. Once again, Coloradans worked to attract the new transportation system. On May 31, 1925, 10,000 people gathered in a vacant field in east Denver.

They cheered as a World War I biplane slowly lifted off the ground carrying 325 pounds of mail (13,000 letters). It was the first airmail flight out of Denver. Three years later Western Air Express began carrying passengers as well as the mail.

Frontier Airlines, Colorado's largest home state airline, traces its roots to Monarch Airlines, founded in 1946 with passenger flights from Denver to Durango. Monarch merged in 1950 with Challenger Airlines of Denver and Arizona Airways to become Frontier Airlines. By the 1980s, Frontier flew to a half dozen Colorado towns and almost 100 cities in the United States, Canada, and Mexico.

The 1929 dedication of Stapleton International Airport (then Denver Municipal Airport) with an Army National Guard Douglas Observation Plane coming in for a landing. The pilot occupied the front cockpit while the observer sat in the back with binoculars and a machine gun.
—Erwin Krebs Collection

Aspen Airways, Pioneer Airways, Rocky Mountain Airways, and Trans Colorado Airlines also connect Colorado cities. Dozens of national and international airlines serve Colorado. The story of Robert F. Six is probably the best-known Colorado legend of the skyways. In 1936, Six took over Continental Airlines. When he retired forty-four years later as president of Continental, it had become one of America's biggest airlines and had moved its headquarters to Los Angeles.

Colorado's isolation from major cities and the east and west coast population centers ended with the arrival of the airlines. Colorado is now only a few hours away from San Francisco and New York and only a day or two away from anywhere in the world. By the 1980s, Stapleton International Airport was one of the five busiest airports in America.

Airplanes and automobiles have largely solved Colorado's old problem of geographic isolation. Thanks in part to the automobile and the airplane, Colorado has become a popular place both to visit and to live.

DID YOU KNOW:

- That 69% of Colorado rain falls on the Western Slope?
- That Colorado has the highest paved auto route in the country—the road to the top of Mount Evans.
- That work began on Interstate 25 in 1948 and on Interstate 70 in 1957.
- That the Eisenhower Tunnel on Interstate 70 is 1.693 miles long and is 9.1 miles shorter than the old Loveland Pass route.
- That the Regional Transportation District (RTD or The Ride) includes what used to be the Denver Tramway Company.

QUESTIONS:

1. Why are water projects so important in Colorado?

2. List some of the projects that have shifted Western Slope water to other areas of Colorado. Do any of these projects affect your water supply?

3. List three changes in communication and three changes in transportation in Colorado in the 1920s.

4. How did the automobile affect the economy of Colorado?

5. What are the leading tourist attractions in your county?

6. Why were both railroads and airlines slow to put routes through Colorado?

ACTIVITIES:

1. As a class project, research your town's water resources. Where does your water come from? How is it stored? What problems concerning water are important to your community?

2. Study business directories in your community at the turn of the century. Locate the saloons or hotels. Based on this information, do you think that your community had laws controlling the sale of alcohol before prohibition?

3. The automobile greatly affected the state of Colorado. Look at advertisements for automobiles in old newspapers to discover the models, prices, and the dealerships for automobiles in your community.

4. Pretend you are going to establish a new factory in your town. Decide what your product will be and then research the means of transportation you will use to get your product to market.

Books you might enjoy:

Gene Fowler. *Timber Line*. New York: Covici-Friede, 1933. Funny, best-selling tale of Denver and the *Denver Post*.

Miller, Jeff. *Stapleton International Airport*, Boulder, Pruett Publishing Company, 1983.

Muriel S. Wolle. *Stampede to Timberline: The Ghost Towns and Mining Camps of Colorado*. Denver: Sage Books, 1949. The best guide to ghost towns.

W.P.A. Writers Program. *Colorado: A Guide to the Highest State*. 2nd rev. ed. New York: Hastings House, 1970. The best guide to living towns.

—15—
Depression, War & The Federal Government

For every boom there is usually a bust. Colorado's silver boom ended with the Panic of 1893. The good times of the 1920s ended with the Great Depression, which began in 1929 with the crash of the New York Stock Exchange. Stock values collapsed and many companies went out of business. Recovery came very slowly and only after the federal government spent billions of dollars to put people back to work.

Even people who had saved their money in banks were hurt by the Great Depression. In Colorado, 66 of the state's 237 banks failed during the 1930s. For a time, all banks were closed so that the federal government could determine which ones had enough money to reopen. After the stronger banks reopened, the federal government promised to insure deposits. This program, the Federal Deposit Insurance Corporation, is still in effect. It means that if a bank fails, the government will pay depositors whatever they had in it, up to $100,000.

Even worse than losing stocks and bank savings, many people lost their jobs. In 1933, about a quarter of all Americans were out of work, including thousands of Coloradans. No longer did people talk about buying cars and new houses, they just hoped for enough to eat. They hunted jackrabbits for stews, captured coyotes for the $5 per head bounty, and panned for gold.

During the Great Depression of the 1930s, junk collectors like this one haunted Colorado's cities. They collected old bottles, cans, cardboard, newspapers, rags and other trash for recycling.
—Denver Post

Young people who could once afford to rent their own apartments moved back into their parents' homes. Grandparents, aunts and uncles moved in with their relatives. Many families planted vegetable gardens and raised rabbits, chickens, pigs and goats to save on the grocery bill.

In depression-hit neighborhoods such as the Grove in Pueblo and Globeville in Denver, some children broke the law so their families could survive. For example, they crawled under parked railroad grain cars to drill holes in the car bottoms and let the wheat run into bags which they took home to their mothers for bread-making.

The Depression was especially hard on retired older people without families to rely on. The poorest of them could be seen poking around in garbage cans for food and clothing. If they had a little money, they would shop at the many pawn shops, flea markets, and second hand stores that popped up during the 1930s. To help the elderly poor, the state of Colorado set up an old age pension plan. It paid needy persons aged sixty or over $45 a month, using money from taxes on liquor (which became legal again in 1933) and other items. A few years later, President Franklin D. Roosevelt and Congress set up the Social Security system to aid the old and the helpless.

Blacks and Mexican Americans also suffered. For example, in Five Points, Denver's black neighborhood, Benny Hooper turned his night club into a soup line. People who had dined and danced at Hooper's Casino in the 1920s lined up there in the 1930s for jackrabbit stew. Benny ran the stewline with the same hospitality that had made his Welton Street nightclub one of the hottest clubs of the 1920s.

Agriculture

Farmers were among the hardest hit victims of the Depression. They found it cost more to raise their crops and animals than they sold for on the market. Apples that had previously sold for $1.45 a bushel brought only $.42 a bushel. Pigs that had sold for $12 in 1929 sold for $3 at the bottom of the Depression in 1933. Wheat prices fell from $.96 a bushel to $.37. Many people lost their farms and moved into cities.

To survive, farmers began to work together. During the 1920s, the Monte Vista Potato Growers' Cooperative and the United Fruit Growers Association of Palisade had shown the advantages of cooperation. Soon farmers all over the state began forming Co-ops. These organizations enabled farmers to pool their money to buy farm machinery and build grain elevators that could be shared. Today, as you travel around Colorado, look for the Co-op grain elevators. They are the biggest landmarks in many farm towns, larger even than the water tanks.

Farmers also continued to try dry land farming. This means growing crops that do not need much water—crops such as winter wheat—and plowing deeply and weeding carefully to conserve the available water. By these methods and by taking advantage of winter snows, dry farms can prosper without irrigation. Colorado State University at Fort Collins also helped farmers by developing drought-resistant varieties of wheat, corn, and other crops.

Even the best dry land farming techniques, however, were of little use in the drought and dust storms that swept the

During the 1920s and 1930s, farmers formed co-ops to build grain elevators like these for wheat in Holyoke, Colorado. —Photo by Tom Noel

Great Plains during the 1930s. LeRoy Hafen, a famous historian of Colorado, wrote in his journal on April 10, 1935:

> We had our second dust storm over Denver. It was almost suffocating. Part of the night I slept with a wet towel over my face to strain the dust . . . .

If anything green survived the drought and the "black blizzards," it often was eaten by the grasshopper plagues that added to farmers' woes during the 1930s.

Some Colorado mines reopened in the 1930s when Uncle Sam began buying a lot of gold and silver at a good price. Dredge mining was done around Breckenridge, Central City and Fairplay. Today, you can see the remains of this mining monster in French Gulch near Breckenridge.
—Photo by Tom Noel

Colorado, along with the rest of America, sank into poverty. In such troubled times, it is comforting to at least have someone to pin the blame on; angry voters threw the Republicans out of office and elected mostly Democrats during the 1930s.

Senator Costigan

Edward P. Costigan was chosen for one of the U.S. Senate seats. He was a small, dark man whose mother was Spanish. This made him popular with Colorado's Mexican-American voters. Costigan, a lawyer educated at Harvard, entered politics after being physically assaulted for complaining about illegal voting. As a result, Costigan became a champion of reform. He worked with Judge Ben Lindsey, ran for governor of Colorado on the Progressive Party slate in 1912, and helped Josephine Roche run for governor in 1934.

In 1932, Senator Costigan worked for the election of Franklin D. Roosevelt as president of the United States. Roosevelt promised a "New Deal" for the poor, the elderly, small farmers and business people, and minority groups.

The New Deal also helped miners. After passing the Silver Purchase Act of 1934, the government began buying up all the silver that could be mined for $1.29 an ounce. Washington also began buying gold at $35.00 an ounce. Old mines began to reopen and miners went back to work.

The WPA and the CCC

The largest New Deal program, the Works Progress Administration (WPA), spent over $110 million in Colorado and provided work for about 150,000 people. The unemployed were hired by this Federal agency to build roads and bridges, schools and libraries, ball fields and swimming pools, sewers and airports. A new high school in Clifton, a giant water tower in Walsh, and a golf course in Greeley were among the thousands of WPA projects in Colorado. The WPA also set up a drama program for out-of-work actors, actresses, and playwrights and created a Federal Writers Project that employed out-of-work writers to produce a guidebook to Colorado.

Young people between the ages of eighteen and twenty-five found jobs with another New Deal program, the Civilian Conservation Corps (CCC). The CCC paid unemployed youths $1 a day to build hiking trails and campgrounds, to fight forest fires and make dams, and to do many other jobs in the national forests and parks. Red Rocks outdoor theatre near Denver, Flagstaff Mountain road near Boulder, a dormitory for Ute Indians at Ignacio, and the Winter Park ski area were among the many CCC projects. Whenever you enjoy the outdoors in Colorado, you may well be fishing in a lake that the CCC dammed, camping at a shelter it erected, or driving over back-roads it built.

Colorado ranchers were enthusiastic about another New Deal idea. The Taylor Grazing Act was named for Representative Edward Taylor of Glenwood Springs. Under this act, livestock owners were charged a small fee for grazing their animals on federal lands. This fee was used to build watering places and to fence and maintain the land. Another Coloradan, rancher Farrington R. Carpenter of Hayden, went to Washington to get the grazing plan started. Thanks in part to Taylor and Carpenter, this federal program still works today.

World War II

Although the federal government spent billions to end the Great Depression, not everybody found work and industry did not really prosper until America entered World War II in 1941. American workers made weapons and supplies, not only for our own armed forces but also for those of Great Britain, France, Russia, and our other allies. Farmers and ranchers began to do well again also, for Colorado beef, lamb, and pork, as well as wheat and sugar, fed people all over a warring world.

With 138,832 Coloradans fighting in World War II, manpower became short at home. So during World War II America used one of its most overlooked resources—womanpower. Women worked in factories, ran farms and ranches, drove buses and managed businesses. Even the old superstition that women in mines would bring bad luck was disproved. The war gave women a chance to prove that they could do "man's work."

Wartime shortages also taught Coloradans to recycle everything from car tires to newspapers. Four-H Clubs, scout troops, church groups and civic clubs helped support the war effort by selling war bonds and stamps, by collecting millions of tons of old newspapers, scrap iron, and steel, rubber, tin cans, bottles and even kitchen fats that were usually thrown in the garbage can. Families also learned to grow their own vegetables in "Victory Gardens."

World War II changed Colorado's economy. Vanadium, molybdenum, and tungsten were mined to help make steel. After the United States introduced the nuclear age by bombing Hiroshima and Nagasaki in Japan, the Western Slope became

Even children joined Colorado's World War II effort. Ranchers and farmers were busy helping to feed the troops.
—*Amon Carter Museum*

a prime region for mining and processing radium and uranium used for nuclear weapons, power plants, and medicine. Unfortunately, the mining, milling, and processing of these radioactive materials have left hazardous wastes that can cause health problems.

Military bases and hospitals built during the two world wars are still very important to Colorado's economy. Fort Carson near Colorado Springs, Lowry Air Force Base in Denver, Fitzsimons Army Medical Center in Aurora, and other military installations pump millions of dollars into Colorado by hiring local people and buying local supplies.

Spin-offs from other military projects have changed Colorado in many ways. Camp Hale near Leadville is a good example. During World War II, the U.S. Army trained soldiers in ski warfare there. For fun on weekends, the soldiers skied around the old silver city of Aspen. After the war, some of these soldiers remembered the sparkling powder snow and the scenic slopes surrounding this quiet mining town. They came back and helped convert a near ghost town into the world famous Aspen ski resort. Later some of the Camp Hale veterans helped lay out some of the three dozen other ski areas that now make Colorado America's most popular spot for winter sports.

The Post War Boom

The federal government's large projects and paychecks brought Colorado out of the Depression during the 1940s. And after World War II ended in 1945, many army and air force veterans stationed in Colorado during the war decided to move here. For example, Aurora in 1940 was a small farm town with a population of 3,437. By the 1980s, however, Aurora had become Colorado's third largest city with a population approaching 200,000.

Lakewood in Jefferson County is another modern-day boom town. During World War II, a giant weapons factory was set up there. After the war ended, this complex became the Federal Center, housing many of the government offices that have given the Denver metropolitan area the nickname of "Little Washington, D.C." Thanks in part to thousands of government jobs at the Federal Center, Lakewood has grown into the fourth largest city in Colorado.

Colorado's 63 Counties
How many have you visited?

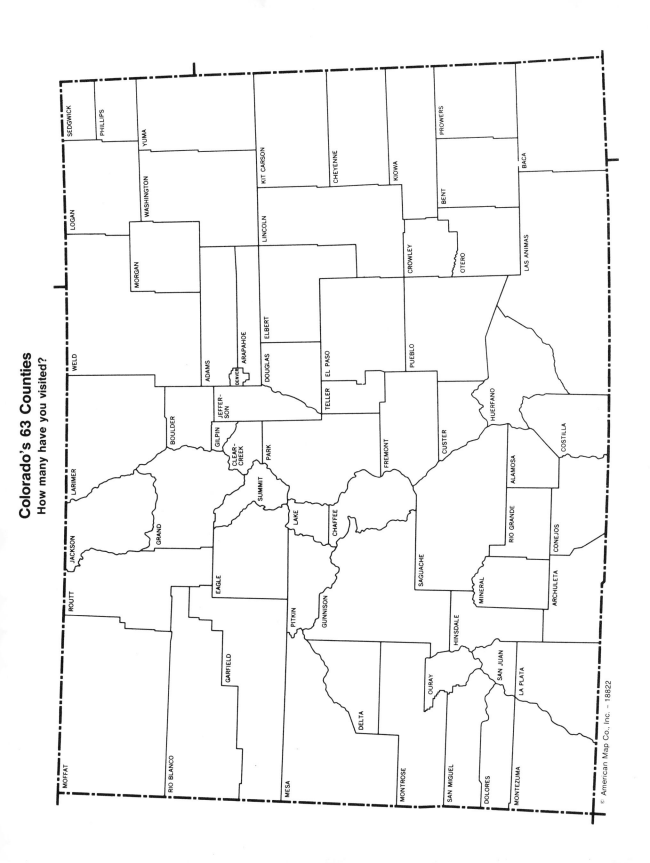

Since 1945, Colorado has become one of America's fastest growing states. After relatively slow growth between the Crash of 1893 and World War II, our state has boomed in recent decades, as the following chart shows:

COLORADO POPULATION

1900:	539,700	1950:	1,325,089
1910:	799,024	1960:	1,753,947
1920:	939,629	1970:	2,207,259
1930:	1,035,791	1980:	2,888,964
1940:	1,123,296	1990:	3,480,477 (estimate)

By the 1980s, newcomers outnumbered natives in many areas. After two world wars and the Great Depression, our state has enjoyed a boom similar to the gold and silver booms of the 1870s and 1880s. As we shall see, however, not everyone has shared in the post war boom.

DID YOU KNOW:

- Nine out of ten Coloradans live on the eastern slope.
- Coloradans created four tons of trash per minute in 1969.
- Only 41% of Colorado residents are natives (1980 census).
- Nine Colorado counties had no doctors in 1976: Denver had 2290.
- In 1970, 31 of Colorado's 63 counties had fewer people than in 1900.

QUESTIONS:

1. If another depression strikes Colorado, what are some of the ways you could help your family find food, shelter, and clothing?
2. What was the CCC? How did it open up Colorado's back country for recreation?
3. Ask some of the older people in your town or your grandparents about their lives during the Great Depression.
4. How did World War II speed up Colorado's growth?
5. Why is Denver sometimes called "Little Washington, D.C."?

ACTIVITIES:

1. Look around your town for bridges, schools, parks, and other public works. See if they have a WPA (Works Progress Administration) sign and a date on them.
2. Call the oldest bank in your community and ask if your class can take a field trip there. You might ask the bank president how his or her bank would deal with a depression.
3. Make a chart showing your town's growth since 1900.
4. List some of the federal offices in your county. You can find them in the phone book under United States Government.
5. Check into your local recycling programs. How many things that people usually throw away can be collected and sold for cash?

Books you might enjoy:

David Lavender. *One Man's West*, 2nd, rev. ed. Garden City, N.Y.: Doubleday & Co., Inc., 1956. A first rate account of how western Colorado is faring in the twentieth century, including a final chapter about "uranium on the cranium."

Ostis Otto Moore. *Mile High Harbor*. Denver: Associated Pubs., 1947. A firsthand account of Colorado's old age pension plan by Judge Moore, who spearheaded the drive for this pioneer plan.

Gerald S. Nash. *The American West in the Twentieth Century*. Englewood Cliffs, N.J.: Prentice- Hall, Inc., 1973.

Sprague, Marshall. *Newport in the Rockies: The Life and Good Times of Colorado Springs*. Athens, Ohio, Swallow Press, 1971.

—16—
Economic and Ethnic Diversity

Charles Boettcher left Germany for America when he was seventeen. He hopped off the Union Pacific train at Cheyenne, Wyoming, for a visit with his brother Herman, who ran a hardware store. Herman put his little brother to work in the store, paying him a dollar or two a week and letting him sleep under the counter at night.

When Colorado began to grow in the 1870s, the Boettcher brothers decided to open branch stores there. Charles built the two-story brick store that still stands at Pearl and Broadway in Boulder. A few years later, Charles moved to Leadville and started another hardware store. By 1890, he had moved to Denver to start still another business.

Boettcher was smart. He saw his friends put all their money into one mine, one business, or one railroad. When hard times came, as in 1893 and 1929, they lost everything. Boettcher put his money into many different businesses. That way, if one enterprise failed, he still had the others. Boettcher's approach became Colorado's best example of economic diversity. He created the biggest and richest business empire in Colorado history.

Boettcher loved work more than play, but his wife, Fannie, finally talked him into taking a vacation in Germany. Charles

Margarita Garcia tempts a passerby with South of the Border treats at La Popular, 2012 Larimer, Denver. Mexican food has become a favorite of many Coloradans.
—Roger Whitacre Photo

soon got bored with travel and took his family on a tour of some sugar beet farms, where he saw how the Germans grew the beets and made sugar out of them. Then, according to one story, he made Fannie empty her suitcases so he could fill them with sugar beet seed. He took these back to Colorado and with some friends started the Great Western Sugar Beet Company in 1900. Soon Great Western had fields and factories all over the state.

When Great Western was building its Loveland plant, Charles made an inspection tour. He found that cement for the new plant was being imported from Germany. His engineers told him that they had tried American-made cement and it was not as strong. Charles Boettcher was upset. Why pay such high prices and freight fares when all the materials needed to make cement—lime, silica, and alumina—were available in Colorado? Within a matter of months, Charles set up his own cement company. Today it has evolved into one of Colorado's largest firms—Ideal Basic Industries.

Boettcher invested in railroads, streetcars, the Public Service Company, Capitol Life Insurance Company, meat packing, cattle ranching, a dynamite factory, and dozens of other firms. The Crash of 1929, which bankrupted some of Colorado's millionaires, did not destroy Boettcher. Although some of his various businesses sank during the Depression, others rose in value.

One of Boettcher's buys was Denver's grand old hotel, the Brown Palace, where he lived until his death in 1948. Although he owned the hotel, Charles always refused to buy his soft drinks there. "Too expensive," he said, and walked across the street to a nickel soft drink machine.

Boettcher made his millions in Colorado and he and his son, Claude, decided to return some of it to Coloradans. They created the Boettcher Foundation, which has given over $50 million to Coloradans for college scholarships, for the Boettcher School for the handicapped in Denver, and for hospitals and museums. Claude Boettcher's house in Denver was donated to the state as a governor's mansion, and the Boettcher summer home on Lookout Mountain now houses the Jefferson County Nature Center. The Boettcher Foundation also has given over a million dollars to the Colorado Historical Society, which has museums in Denver, Georgetown, Fort Garland, Fort Vasquez, Leadville, Montrose, Pueblo, and Trinidad.

Charles Boettcher is just one example of how smart business people brought new jobs into Colorado by diversifying the economy. In the 1880s, Coloradans worked mostly in mines and small stores, on farms and ranches, or for railroads and smelters. During the 1890s, the Depression, drought and the silver panic forced people to look for other jobs. Thanks to the efforts of Charles Boettcher and others, Coloradans now work at a wide variety of jobs.

New Business

Since 1950, Colorado has attracted many new businesses. Kodak, the camera and film makers, built a $100 million plant at Windsor near Greeley in the 1970s. Martin-Marietta, an aerospace firm, moved to Littleton in 1955. By the 1980s, Martin-Marietta had 7,500 employees who have built Titan missiles, space satellites and who helped put Americans on the moon. The Storage Technology Corporation of Louisville became Colorado's fastest-growing industry in the 1960s. It was founded by four former IBM employees who set up the business over a Boulder restaurant. By 1980, Storage Technology had over 7,000 employees who designed and sold computer systems all over America.

King Soopers grocery stores and Samsonite Luggage are two other good examples of how small Colorado businesses have flourished. In 1946, Lloyd J. King came back to Denver after serving in the Navy during World War II. He converted a small meat market in Arvada into the first King Soopers grocery store. By 1980, his company had become one of Colorado's leading employers and had stores throughout the state.

Jesse Schwayder, whose Jewish family left Poland for Central City, started making Samsonite luggage in Denver. With the increase in travel and tourism, Samsonite Corporation has added factories in ten other countries and sells its suitcases all over the globe. When someone asked Schwayder why he didn't move his headquarters to a bigger city, he said: "I'd rather make a dollar in Denver than three dollars in New York."

In the 1970s, the Anaconda and Johns-Manville companies both moved their headquarters from New York City to Denver. Anaconda moved into a forty-four-story building on Denver's Seventeenth Street, known as "the Wall Street of the Rockies." Johns-Manville, which makes roofing and building materials,

Charles Boettcher, who came to Colorado from Germany as a teenager, became rich and famous in many different fields of business.
—*Tom Noel Collection*

built a huge new building on the old Ken-Caryl Ranch in the foothills west of Littleton. There transplanted New York executives can see nesting eagles and herds of deer from their office windows.

Tourism, another major industry, has become a year-round money-maker. In the old days, tourists just came in the summer. Now winter and spring skiing bring millions of guests to "Ski Country, U.S.A.," and fall aspen tours have been promoted to lure visitors during September and October. In the 1940s, Colorado began advertising, "spend one more day in Colorado." By the 1970s, the average tourist stayed about eight days.

Hispanos

These visitors to Colorado have found an ethnically diverse population. Spanish-surnamed people were the first Europeans to explore and to settle in Colorado. They gave the state its name. Yet despite being Colorado's largest ethnic group and despite a proud heritage, they have sometimes been treated as second-class citizens.

Since the 1960s, Hispanos have been fighting harder to improve their lives in Colorado. Foremost among the militant Chicanos has been Rudolfo "Corky" Gonzales, who was born in Denver in 1928. As a young man, Gonzales was a professional boxer. Since the 1960s, however, he has been fighting for *La Raza* (the Hispanic people). Gonzales is also a poet who wrote about the experiences of his people:

> Here I stand,
> poor in money,
> arrogant with pride,
> . . . My knees are caked with mud.
> My hands calloused from the hoe.
> I have made the Anglo rich . . .

Hispanos helped create Colorado. Nine served in the early state legislature, representing southern Colorado. Later, when Spanish-surnamed people began to leave southern Colorado and settle all over the state, they lost political representation. Today, about seventy-five percent of the state's Hispanos live in the Denver, Pueblo, Greeley, and Colorado Springs areas. Around 100,000 Hispanos live in Denver, where they form a fifth of the city's population. Statewide, the 1980 census counted 339,300 Spanish-surnamed Coloradans, or nearly twelve percent of the population.

Most communities now have successful Hispanic teachers, business people, and politicians. Cecil J. Hernandez is a good example. In the 1950s he started a one-man cabinet company in Denver. By 1980, Hernandez's Mastercraft Cabinet Company had become the eleventh largest in the United States with two shops in Denver, one in Loveland, and another in Phoenix, Arizona. Mastercraft cabinets are sold all over the West, from Wisconsin to California, from Dallas, Texas, to Spokane, Washington. His firm became the largest minority-owned business in Colorado.

Hispanos are learning the keys to economic and political opportunity—education, registering to vote, and voting. By 1980, there were nine Hispanos in the Colorado State Legislature. A Hispano served as mayor of Pueblo and two sat on the Denver City Council. In 1983, Federico Peña was elected mayor of Denver. As Colorado's fastest-growing and largest minority, Hispanos look forward to even more political and economic gains.

Blacks

Most of Colorado's black residents live in Denver. This Afro-American community is one of the richest and best educated in America with an income higher than the average for all Americans. Sixty-eight percent of Denver's blacks own their own homes and almost half of them own two cars. The average black in Denver has had at least a year of college.

But, blacks have had to struggle to do well. For years they were concentrated in the old Five Points neighborhood just north of downtown Denver. In the 1950s, however, some blacks wanted bigger and better homes.

They began moving across Colorado Boulevard into the Park Hill neighborhood, which has beautiful, tree-shaded, big old homes. Whites who were afraid of these new people tried to sell their houses. Sometimes much of a block would have "For Sale" signs. Because blacks and whites did not know or trust each other, they were afraid to live near each other.

Churches in Park Hill decided to do something. They helped set up what has become the Greater Park Hill Community, Inc. This group introduced black newcomers to the old white

Big Daddy Bruce of Denver is famous for the dinners he serves for the Denver Broncos. He also give a huge free picnic for poor people every year. Have you ever tasted barbecued ribs like the one on the end of Big Daddy's stick?
—*Roger Whitacre Photo*

residents. They held block parties, gave picnics, put out a newspaper and helped people to realize that whites and blacks could live in the same block, go to the same school, use the same playgrounds and pray in the same churches.

Park Hill has become a success story. Blacks call it "Struggle Hill" because of their struggle to get there. Whites call it proof that Americans can rise above the racial prejudices of the past. And nationally, Park Hill is called one of the best integrated neighborhoods in the United States.

These Japanese children are trying out a new way to get around. Why are many of Colorado's Japanese citizens found in the South Platte and Arkansas River Valleys? —Denver Post

Japanese-Coloradans

Few Japanese came to Colorado before 1900. After 1900 they were asked to come to Colorado to work in the sugar beet fields that Charles Boettcher and others were promoting. Most of these newcomers settled near the sugar beet farms along the Arkansas and South Platte River valleys.

Wages were low, but the Japanese carefully saved whatever money they could. Whole families would spend the day planting, weeding and harvesting sugar beets, but early in the morning and late at night they tended their own vegetable patches. Slowly, many Japanese saved enough cash to buy their own farms or to move into towns and start small businesses.

In 1941, Japan bombed Pearl Harbor in Hawaii, the Pacific base for the United States Navy. Following this, the United States declared war on Japan and entered World War II. At that time there were almost 3,000 Japanese-Americans in Colorado. Their number was soon to grow, because the United States government, in a wartime panic, rounded up all the Japanese in California, Oregon, and Washington. Although these people were loyal American citizens, some people thought they would help Japan attack the West Coast.

The Japanese were put in relocation camps away from the West Coast. One camp, Amache, was built near the little town of Granada along the Arkansas River in southeastern Colorado. Tiny babies and very old ladies were among the 8,000 Japanese sent there. Overnight, it became one of the largest towns in Colorado. Many of the men volunteered to fight for the United States to prove their patriotism. The Japanese-American combat troops earned more medals for bravery than any other group fighting in World War II and many of them gave their lives for America.

Some Coloradans wanted to lock up the Colorado Japanese with those in the concentration camp at Granada. Governor Ralph Carr, however, pointed out that they were loyal Americans, just like the German-Americans who were loyal to the United States and not to the German leader, Adolph Hitler. Governor Carr refused to jail Japanese-Coloradans, and after the war the Japanese honored the governor who had defended them. They put a statue of Governor Carr in Sakura Square, the center of Denver's Japanese district.

Ethnic Diversity

Coloradans are many people. They are Indians and Spanish, French and English, German and Irish. Some are Jews from Russia, others are Moslems from the Middle East. Italians, Greeks, and Slavs have settled in the Centennial State, as have Swiss and Scandinavians. People have come to Colorado from all corners of the world.

Southeast Asians have been among the latest immigrants.

They started coming in the 1970s, fleeing wars in Vietnam, Laos, and Cambodia. After getting used to a land where there is both snow and cactus, where there are both big cities and wide open, empty spaces, many of these people have come to like Colorado. By studying hard in school and working hard in jobs, many are doing well in America. These Asian-Americans, like early immigrants, have usually found that Coloradans are a big-hearted, friendly people. Most Coloradans realize that the diversity of people, like the diversity of jobs, makes our state richer and more interesting.

QUESTIONS:

1. Why did Charles Boettcher start many different kinds of businesses?

2. What different kinds of jobs are done in your county? Would you say it has a diversified economy?

3. How has the Boettcher Foundation helped Colorado? What wealthy people in your area have helped out the community? How?

4. What ethnic groups live in your town? Do they fight or work together?

5. Do you think it was fair to lock up the Japanese at Camp Amache near Granada during World War II?

6. What makes Denver's Park Hill neighborhood special?

ACTIVITIES:

1. Take a tour of the biggest factories in your county. Ask the president of the factory if they have diversified.

2. Visit your town hall or chamber of commerce and ask them what the biggest tourist attractions are in your community.

3. Take a bus tour of the richest and the poorest neighborhoods in your area. What are the biggest differences between them?

4. Ask your parents about the countries from which your ancestors came. Does your family have anything from the old country? Any foods, songs, or traditions? Share your ethnic background with your classmates.

5. Organize a class trip to one of the ethnic restaurants in your area. Have everyone order a different ethnic food so you can try them all.

Books you might enjoy:

Geraldine Bean. *Charles Boettcher: A Study in Pioneer Western Enterprise*. Boulder, Colorado: Westview Press, 1976.

Rodolfo Gonzales. *I Am Joaquin*. New York: Bantam Books, 1972.

Bill Hosokowa. *Thirty-five Years in the Frying Pan*. New York: McGraw-Hill, 1978. One of several books on Japanese Americans by an editor of the *Denver Post* who spent World War II in a relocation camp.

Junior Reading

Eleanor Ayer. *Hispanic Colorado*. Frederick, Colorado: Jende-Hagan Bookcorp, 1982. (The Colorado Chronicles, Volume 4.)

Suzanne Thumhart. *Colorado Businesses*. Frederick, Colorado: Jende-Hagan Bookcorp, 1983. (The Colorado Chronicles, Volume 6.)

—17—
Conserving Colorado

Colorado celebrated its 100th birthday as a state in 1976, while the United States celebrated its 200th birthday. Some Coloradans found 1976 a good time to look back at the first 100 years and think about their history.

The biggest change was in the number of people. In 1876 there were about 100,000 Coloradans. In 1976 there were over 2 million, with 3 million expected by 1990. In 1876, thousands of Indians still lived in Colorado. In 1976, there were only a few left, mostly on two small Ute Reservations in the southwestern corner of the state and in Denver.

The 1859 gold rush brought over 25,000 fortune seekers into Colorado. These new Coloradans—the miners and townspeople, farmers and ranchers—went to work like beavers. They built dams and ditches to provide water for their mines and towns, their farms and factories. The settlers said nature's flow had to be changed to accommodate people.

Many early Coloradans did not like the mountains. To them, the Rocky Mountains were only rock that hid gold and silver, coal and oil, marble and granite. So the mountains were blasted and dug and tunneled for mines, wagon roads, railroads, and auto roads.

A huddle of new high rises now stands at 17th St. and Broadway in the heart of downtown Denver.
—Roger Whitacre Photo

Nature's Revenge

Nature gave a few warning signs. After trees were cut down, snow melted much faster and ran off quickly. Floods rolled into the towns. Because trees along the headwaters of the Arkansas River around Leadville had been cut down, the river flooded Pueblo in 1921. A wall of water killed 100 people and carried away horses, wagons, cars, and even railroad cars as if they were toys. After these floods, Coloradans built more dams. But even the new dams did not always hold. Castlewood Dam broke in 1933 and Cherry Creek flooded Denver. Colorado's waterways have continued to break through dams and channels. In 1976, nearly twelve inches of rain fell in four hours on the Big Thompson River Canyon. The river rose nineteen feet above its normal level and roared down the canyon from Estes Park to Loveland. This was the worst flood in Colorado history, killing 145 people and destroying 418 homes and 52 businesses.

In 1982, another flood left Coloradans feeling uneasy because so many towns lie below dammed up water. Lawn Lake Dam burst in Rocky Mountain National Park. The roaring flood did not stop until it had buried the main street of Estes Park in mud and water. Some thought the answer was to build bigger and better dams. Others argued that Colorado already had too many dams and said we should try to live more in harmony with nature the way the Indians did. These people are called conservationists, or environmentalists.

Conservation or Development?

The fight between conservationists and developers is not new. Remember Enos Mills and his fight to create Rocky Mountain National Park? President Theodore Roosevelt also fought to reserve small parts of Colorado as national parks and forests. Enos Mills and Theodore Roosevelt argued that parts of the western wilderness should be preserved for future generations. Mountains, Mills argued, would make Colorado a tourist attraction. Why keep tearing down the mountains, chopping and burning the forests, and polluting and diverting the streams? Mills urged Coloradans to enjoy the high country. Ski the snowy slopes, fish the icy streams. Hike into virgin blue spruce forests and camp under the stars. Why not look for wild flowers instead of gold, and hunt with a camera instead of a gun?

Colorado's rapid growth in the 1950s, 1960s, and 1970s worried some people. They saw the number of large-scale developers grow from 30 in 1960 to over 1,000 by 1980. Fortune seekers prowled the state, looking for "unspoiled" areas where they could build resorts and summer homes, suburbs and shopping centers. Hundreds of developments sprang up all over Colorado.

The threat of overdevelopment concerned enough Coloradans that in 1972 a statewide vote was taken to decide whether Colorado should host the 1976 Winter Olympics.

Those who favored holding this famous international sporting competition in Colorado believed it would bring people and money to Colorado from all over the world. Other Coloradans thought there were already enough winter resorts and development in the mountains. The Olympic games would mean more traffic jams, more "NO TRESPASSING" signs, and less chance to find peace and quiet in the high country. Still others asked who would pay for the Olympics. Slowly, people began to suspect that Colorado taxpayers would pay many of the bills while others made the money.

Taxpayers began organizing a revolt in the early 1970s after Colorado politicians and business people said that the Olympics would be held at all costs. When the leaders refused to listen, Colorado citizens drew up a petition forbidding the state of Colorado to spend any more money on the 1976 Winter Olympics. Over 76,000 voters signed the petition, and it went on the ballot in the fall of 1972. Two out of every three voters said no to the Winter Olympics.

Politically, the 1972 revolt was also a turning point. Many politicians were replaced during the next few years, including the governor, both U.S. senators, and three U.S. representatives. Usually they lost to candidates who promised to do more to protect the environment and to control growth.

Women played an important part in the conservation movement and in politics. They became a common sight in the state legislature. Denverites elected Pat Schroeder to the U.S. House of Representatives and she was re-elected by big margins. Mary Estill Buchanan became the first female Secretary of State, and Nancy Dick of Aspen became Colorado's first female Lieutenant Governor.

Georgetown, an old silver mining town, has kept many of its old buildings, including this fire tower. Why were fires such a problem in mountain mining towns?
—*Ira Gay Sealy Photo*

Historic Preservation

Centennial celebrations in 1976 made Colorado towns more aware of their history. People began to look around for historic old railroad stations, stores, hotels, schools, homes and churches. Most of them were gone. During the postwar boom, thousands of old buildings were knocked down. In Denver, they even used dynamite to blow away buildings until people complained about the dust and the danger.

Some people began to worry about how fast Colorado's historical buildings were being demolished. Concerned residents formed a group called Historic Denver, Inc., which grew into one of the largest preservation societies in the United States by the 1980s. Among Historic Denver's accomplishments have been the saving of the Molly Brown House in Denver's old Capitol Hill neighborhood. "Unsinkable" Molly Brown's house is now a museum drawing thousands of visitors each year. Families also come to Denver to see the United States Mint, the Colorado Heritage Center, the Denver Art Museum, the Children's Museum, the Denver Museum of Natural History, the Denver Zoo, and restored historic neighborhoods such as Curtis Park, Auraria, Capitol Hill, and Highlands.

Other Colorado cities have also set aside areas for preservation. Mapleton Avenue in Boulder, Main Street in Littleton, Main Avenue in Durango, Main Street in Sterling, Old Town in Fort Collins, and Pitkin Place in Pueblo are among the elegant survivors from the 19th century.

Georgetown, Colorado's first silver city, has been the star of the state when it comes to historic preservation. Since 1970, this little town snuggled in a mountain valley boasts that it has not lost one of over 200 historic buildings.

Georgetown set up one of Colorado's first historic districts. Then the Georgetown Society began raising money to repair old houses. When a developer started to build new condominiums on the Guanella Pass Road, this tiny town of around 1,000 people committed over $500,000 to buy out the developer in order to preserve Georgetown's historic charm.

Other famous old mining towns also decided to restore buildings from their past to improve their quality of life and attract tourists. Now Central City, Crested Butte, Cripple Creek, Lake City, Leadville, Morrison, Silverton, and Telluride

After rowing away from the sinking ocean liner Titanic, Molly Brown was called "Unsinkable". Her house at 1340 Pennsylvania Street in Denver is now a favorite stop for tourists.
—Colorado Historical Society

are historic districts. They strive to keep the flavor of the old days. New development is permitted only if the projects are kept small and look like the rest of the town. Old buildings are recycled into new restaurants, hotels, art galleries, shops, museums, and theaters.

Return of The Railroads

Colorado's railroads have also drawn the attention of preservationists. Once there were over 100 railroads operating in the Centennial State. By the 1980s, there were only five major lines left—AMTRAK, the Burlington Northern, Rio Grande, Santa Fe, and Union Pacific. Some rail fans wanted to restore the old narrow gauge lines (a railroad track only 3' wide instead of the standard 4'8½"). The Durango-Silverton train's popularity inspired the states of Colorado and New Mexico to begin operating another passenger train between Antonito and Chama, New Mexico. You can also take train rides up Pike's Peak, at Cripple Creek, at Heritage Square near Golden, on the AMTRAK Zephyr between Denver and Salt Lake City, and at the Colorado Railroad Museum in Golden. In 1982, the Boettcher Foundation gave the Colorado Historical Society $1 million to complete its restoration of the Georgetown-Silver Plume loop. Some day you may be able to tour Colorado the way your grandparents did—by rail.

Your Future

By the 1980s, Coloradans could look back upon an exciting history, a history more colorful and dramatic than any television show or movie. But it is largely a drama that you will have to discover for yourself by traveling around the state, by reading and by asking older people to tell their stories.

Colorado's people have been industrious, but also reckless and destructive. Not until the 1970s did many Coloradans realize that they were using up the mountains and the plains, the fresh air and the clean water. Colorado, once a health resort for the nation, now suffers from too much pollution and, some say, too many people. Others have been concerned about radioactive wastes and the manufacture of nuclear weapons in the state. How can we brag about Colorado when Denver has some of the dirtiest air in America and it is not safe to drink out of mountain streams?

What will Colorado be like in 2076? Coal and oil, sought by modern miners, cannot be replaced. Will future Coloradans find coal and oil ghost towns? A shortage of water may have driven the Indians out of their great cities at Mesa Verde. Some think the same problem may also cause our biggest cities to dry up and become deserted.

The old narrow gauge line between Antonito, Colorado and Chama New Mexico returned to passenger service in 1971 as the Cumbres & Toltec Scenic Railroad. Why are railroads a popular way to tour Colorado?
—Tom Noel Collection

Yet Coloradans have been a hopeful people. After celebrating the 100th birthday in 1976, many became more interested in preserving the state's history and conserving its natural resources. Perhaps you will not be around in 2076, but your children will be. And they will be looking for the same thing we are—blue skies and clear water, unspoiled mountains to play in, and well-preserved towns to live in. In 2076, they will judge how well we have conserved Colorado.

DID YOU KNOW:

- Keota, with four people, is Colorado's smallest town (1980 census).
- The Eisenhower Tunnel, 8,941 feet long, cost nearly $1,100 per inch to build.
- More tourists come to Colorado from Texas than from anywhere else in the world.
- Colorado has a higher percentage of college graduates than any other state, 23% (1980 census).

QUESTIONS:

1. Look at your town's newspapers for Colorado Day (August 1, 1976). What projects was your community doing to celebrate Colorado's 100th birthday?
2. What are some of the new uses for old buildings in your community?
3. What are modern miners looking for in Colorado?
4. List the narrow gauge railroads that you can ride in Colorado today.
5. What are the historic districts and historic sites in your community?
6. What are the good things about your community that you would like to pass on to your children?

ACTIVITIES:

1. Take a tour of the oldest part of your community. See if there are any nineteenth-century buildings left.

2. Look up your town's newspaper for November of 1972. See what people said in editorials and letters to the editor about holding the 1976 Winter Olympics in Colorado.

3. Ask your local Chamber of Commerce what developments are being planned for your county in the coming years. See if the managers will give a talk to your class on this.

4. Telephone your city or county planning office. Ask them if someone from their office can come give your class a talk on your town's future.

Books you might enjoy:

Colorado Railroad Museum. *The Colorado Rail Annual*. Golden: Colorado Railroad Museum, 1962–present. One of many lavishly illustrated publications on Colorado railroading from the Golden museum.

Mark S. Foster. "Colorado's Defeat of the 1976 Winter Olympics," *The Colorado Magazine*, 53, Spring 1976, pp. 163-186.

David McComb. *Big Thompson: Profile of a Natural Disaster*. Boulder: Pruett Publishing Co., 1980. Professor McComb of CSU has made this a model of oral history.

Thomas J. Noel. *Denver: Rocky Mountain Gold*. Tulsa, Oklahoma: Continental Heritage Press, 1980. A popularly written history with many maps and pictures, some in color.

Duane Vandenbusche and Duane A. Smith. *A Land Alone: Colorado's Western Slope*. Boulder: Pruett Publishing Co., 1981. The definitive account by two of western Colorado's most prolific writers.

Appendix A

Archaeologist's Summary
by
Michael D. Metcalf

The prehistoric people who used Dipper Gap for a camp site were Archaic stage hunters and gatherers. They lived in eastern Colorado and elsewhere on the high plains during a time period called the Plains Archaic. The term "Archaic" is used to describe a way of life as well as to designate a time period. In eastern Colorado the Archaic Stage lasted from about 7500 years ago until about 300 years ago. Charcoal from three of the hearths at Dipper Gap date the main and oldest occupation to about 3000 years ago. Three later archaic groups also used the site, but these levels were not dated by using radiocarbon. Instead, the approximate dates of these later occupations are estimated using the styles of projectile points as indications of age. A general time range is known for certain styles because of dates from other similar sites.

Thus, the date of the four occupations are:
3000–3500 years ago—main occupation
2000–3000 years ago—second occupation
2000–1500 years ago—third occupation
1000– 500 years ago—final occupation

Archaic stage peoples depended on their ability to harvest the naturally occurring foods of the area where they lived.

They did not tend crops or keep domesticated animals such as sheep or cattle. Their diet consisted entirely of the foods they could obtain by gathering, hunting, or fishing. Most Archaic people lived a nomadic lifestyle, moving their camps several times a year as plants and animals became more plentiful elsewhere.

At Dipper Gap we know what some of these foods were, but we can only make guesses about what else they may have eaten. The numerous projectile points, stone arrowheads, and atlatl dart points indicate that these peoples were hunters. An atlatl is a throwing stick used to hurl a short, limber spear or dart. The many stone knives and scrapers are tools used in skinning and butchering game animals after they are killed.

The best indication of what these people hunted comes from bone remains excavated from the twenty-one hearths, or buried remains of cooking fires. Burned and butchered bone from bison was plentiful. Butchered bone from dog, and burned bone of rabbit, antelope, and deer was present as well.

We also guess that various plant foods were collected and used by these peoples. Fragments of the sandstone grinding tools they used to mill these plants were excavated. Grass seeds and other plants were placed on a flat slab known as a *metate*. They were then crushed and ground into a flour using a small cobble called a handstone or *mano*.

In addition to learning about the way people lived in the past by studying the tools from sites, the archaeologist also makes guesses by studying the environment around the site. Dipper Gap is situated near several water sources, but water is only one thing necessary to sustain life. Scientists can study the environment today and make very accurate guesses about what plants and animals would have been there thousands of years ago. At Dipper Gap most of the plant species growing today were also growing during the Archaic period. We know of at least sixty edible plants that now grow near Dipper Gap, but we can only guess at which of these the people were using. A great many animal species, including bison, deer, antelope, elk, bear, mountain lion, and rabbits now live or once lived in the area.

Many Archaic sites are situated in places like Dipper Gap where there is nearby water and access to many species of plants and animals. Archaeologists now know quite a bit about what Archaic people hunted and gathered and where they lived, but we still know very little of what these people thought about, what their ideas and beliefs were. Thoughts and ideas aren't buried and preserved the way hearths, bones, and stones are.

However, at Dipper Gap we do have some clues about one game that might have been played. Six small bone discs were excavated from fill around the remains of a large camp fire. Each of these discs had different markings or lines etched onto its surface. The discs look very much like dominos or dice. We guessed that these discs were used for betting games much the way dice are used now.

In order to find evidence to support this guess a source of information called "Ethnography" was consulted. Ethnography is the study of the lifeways of living groups. Many observations of native American Indians were made by the early explorers of this continent. One man, Stewart Calin, wrote a book called "Games of North American Indians." "Dice" similar to those found at Dipper Gap were used by all of the native cultures he was able to collect information about.

Thus, archaeologists have a sketch of how the Archaic hunters and gatherers of Colorado lived, but certainly we could learn more. New sites studied by archaeologists with more modern methods and equipment will undoubtedly uncover new clues and give us new ideas.

Appendix B
Governors of Colorado

Territorial

William Gilpin, 1861–62
John Evans, 1862–65
Alexander Cummings, 1865–67
A. Cameron Hunt, 1867–69
Edward McCook, 1869–73
Samuel H. Elbert, 1873–74
Edward McCook, 1874–75
John L. Routt, 1875–76

State

John L. Routt (R), 1876–79
Frederick W. Pitkin (R), 1879–83
James B. Grant (D), 1883–85
Benjamin H. Eaton (R), 1885–87
Alva Adams (D), 1887–89
Job A. Cooper (R), 1889–91
John L. Routt (R), 1891–93
Davis H. Waite (P), 1893–95
Albert W. McIntyre (R), 1895–97
Alva Adams (D), 1897–99
Charles S. Thomas (D), 1899–1901
James B. Orman (D), 1901–03

James H. Peabody (R), 1903–05
Alva Adams (D), 1905–
Jesse F. McDonald (R), 1905–07
Henry A. Buchtel (R), 1907–09
John F. Shafroth (D), 1909–13
Elias M. Ammons (D), 1913–15
George A. Carlson (R), 1915–17
Julius C. Gunter (D), 1917–19
Oliver H. Shoup (R), 1919–23
William E. Sweet (D), 1923–25
Clarence J. Morley (R), 1925–27
William H. Adams (D), 1927–33
Edwin C. Johnson (D), 1933–37
Teller Ammons (D), 1937–39
Ralph Carr (R), 1939–43
John Vivian (R), 1943–47
Lee Knous (D), 1947–49
Walter Johnson (D), 1949–51
Dan Thornton (R), 1951–55
Edwin C. Johnson (D), 1955–57
Stephen McNichols (D), 1957–63
John Love (R), 1963–73
John Vanderhoof (R), 1973–75
Richard Lamm (D), 1975–

Sources

Materials used for chapter 1 include:

Walter R. Borneman and Lyndon J. Lampert, *A Climbing Guide to Colorado's Fourteeners*. Boulder: Pruett Publishing, 1978.

David Lavender, *David Lavender's Colorado*. New York: Doubleday, 1976.

Robert Ormes, *Guide to the Colorado Mountains*. Chicago: Sage Press, 1970.

James Grafton Rogers, *My Rocky Mountain Valley*. Boulder: Pruett Press, 1968.

Materials used for chapter 2 include:

Roy G. Coffin, *Northern Colorado's First Settlers*. Fort Collins: Department of Geology, Colorado State College, 1937.

Joe Ben Wheat, "The Olsen-Chubbuck Site, A Paleo-Indian Kill," *Memoirs for the Society for American Archeology,* No. 26, *American Antiquity,* No. 1, Part 2 (January 1972).

Michael D. Metcalf, *Archaeological Excavations at Dipper Gap: A Stratified Butte Top Site in Northeastern Colorado*. Unpublished Master's Thesis, Colorado State University, 1974.

Don Watson, *Indians of Mesa Verde*. Mesa Verde National Park Museum of Natural History, 1961.

Frank McNitt, *Richard Wetherill: Anasazi*. Albuquerque: University of New Mexico Press, 1957.

David Muench and Donald Pike, "Anasazi: Ancient People of the Rock," *National Parkways*. Rocky Mountain and Mesa Verde Issue, 1972.

Materials used for chapter 3 include:

Marvin H. Opler, "A Colorado Ute Indian Bear Dance,": *Southwestern Lore*, Vol. VII:2 (September 1941).

Marvin Opler, "The Southern Utes of Colorado," *Acculturation in Seven Indian Tribes*, New York: D. Appleton-Century Co., 1940.

Scott, "Early History and Names of Arapaho," *American Anthropologist*, N.S., 9, 1907.

George Bird Grinnell, *When Buffalo Ran*. New Haven: Yale University Press, 1920.

Materials for chapter 4 include:

Herbert Averback, "Father Escalante's Journal, 1776–77," *Utah Historical Quarterly,* XI (1943).

Stephen Harding Hart and Archer Butler Hulbert, eds. *Zebulon Pike's Arkansaw Journal*. Denver: Denver Public Library, 1932.

Hiram Chittenden, *The American Fur Trade of the Far West,* Vol. I.

John C. Ewers, ed., *Adventures of Zenas Leonard, Fur Trader*. Norman: University of Oklahoma Press, 1959.

Harvey Lewis Carter, "The Kit Carson Memoirs," *Dear Old Kit, The Historical Christopher Carson,* Norman: University of Oklahoma Press, 1968.

Rufus Sage, *Scenes in the Rocky Mountains*. Glendale, CA: A.H. Clarke Co., 1966.

Materials used for chapter 5 include:

Lewis H. Garrard, *Wah-to-yah and the Taos Trail,* Norman: University of Oklahoma Press, 1955.

George Frederick Ruxton, *Life in the Far West*. LeRoy Hafen, ed. Norman: University of Oklahoma Press, 1951.

LeRoy R. Hafen, "Fort Jackson and the Early Fur Trade on the South Platte," *The Colorado Magazine,* Vol. V (February 1928).

John C. Fremont, *Report of the Exploring Expedition to the Rocky Mountains*. Ann Arbor: University Microfilms, subsidiary of Xerox Corp., 1966.

LeRoy R. Hafen, "Old Fort Lupton and Its Founder," *Colorado Magazine*, Vol. VI: 6 (November 1929).

Materials used for chapter 6 include:

Mrs. S.S. Sanford, "C.W.A. Interview," Colorado State Historical Society Archives.

Horace Greeley, *An Overland Journey from New York to San Francisco in the Summer of 1859,* New York: Knopf, 1964.

William Bent, as quoted in David Lavender, *Bent's Fort,* Garden City: Doubleday, 1954.

William Bent, *Annual Report* of the Commissioner of Indian Affairs, 1859.

Boone to Robinson, April 25, 1861, Upper Arkansas Agency, Letters Received, National Archives, Records of Office of Indian Affairs.

Walter Ennes, "C.W.A. Interview," Colorado State Historical Society Archives.

Elmer R. Burkey, "The Site of the Murder of the Hungate Family by Indians in 1864," *Colorado Magazine,* Vol. XI: 4 (July 1935).

Susan R. Ashley, "Reminiscences of Early Colorado," *Colorado Magazine,* Vol. XIV: 2 (March 1937).

John Evans, "Proclamation," *Rebellion Records,* Series I, Vol. XLI, Part 2.

George Bent, *A Life of George Bent Written From His Letters,* by George E. Hyde, edited by Savoie Lottinville, Norman: University of Oklahoma Press, 1968.

Colonel J.M. Chivington, as reprinted in *The 1963 Brand Book of the Denver Posse,* Denver, 1963.

Major Frank North, "Diary," in Clarence Reckmeyer, "The Battle of Summit Springs," *Colorado Magazine,* Vol. VI: 6 (November 1929).

Margaret Coel, *Chief Left Hand,* Norman: University of Oklahoma Press, 1981.

Indians of Colorado. Frederick, Co: Jende-Hagen Book Corp., 1981. (The Colorado Chronicles: Vol. 3). This Colorado Chronicles series is designed for middle schoolers.

Materials used for chapter 7 include:

Carl Ubbelohde, Maxine Benson, and Duane A. Smith, *A Colorado History*. Boulder: Pruett Publishing, 1982.

Robert Athearn, *The Coloradans*. Albuquerque: University of New Mexico Press, 1976.

Duane A. Smith, *Colorado Mining*. Albuquerque: University of New Mexico Press, 1977.

Muriel S. Wolle, *Stampede to Timberline*. Chicago: Sage, 1974.

Duane A. Smith, *Horace Tabor*. Boulder: Pruett Publishing, 1981. Reprint.

Frank Waters, *Midas of the Rockies*. Chicago: Sage, 1972. Reprint.

Ned Blair, *Leadville*. Boulder, Pruett Publishing, 1980.

Marshall Sprague, *Money Mountain*. Boston: Little, Brown, 1953.

Robert Brown, *Ghost Towns of the Colorado Rockies*. Caldwell: Caxton, 1968.

Materials used for chapter 8 include:

Those in the preceding chapter plus:
Lyle Dorsett, *The Queen City*. Boulder: Pruett Publishing, 1977.

Tom Noel, *Denver: Rocky Mountain Gold*. Tulsa: Continental Heritage Press, 1980.

Isabella Bird, *A Lady's Life in the Rocky Mountains*. Norman: University of Oklahoma Press, 1960. Reprint.

Grace Greenwood (Sara Lippincott), *New Life in New Lands*. New York: J.B. Ford, 1873.

Anne Ellis, *The Life of an Ordinary Woman*. Lincoln: University of Nebraska, 1980. Reprint.

John Dyer, *Snowshoe Itinerant*. Cincinnati: Cranston & Stowe, 1891.

George Darley, *Pioneering in the San Juans*. Lake City: Community Presbyterian Church, 1976. Reprint.

Mabel B. Lee, *Cripple Creek Days*. New York, Doubleday, 1958.

Materials used for chapter 9 include:

Virginia Simmons, *The San Luis Valley*. Boulder: Pruett Publishing, 1979.

Spanish Textile Tradition of New Mexico and Colorado. Santa Fe: Museum of New Mexico, 1979.

Robert Adams, *The Architecture and Art of Early Hispanic Colorado*. Boulder: Colorado Associated University Press, 1974.

Morris Taylor, *Trinidad*. Pueblo: O'Brien, 1966.

Barron Beshoar, *Hippocrates in a Red Vest*. Palo Alto: American West, 1973.

Lee Scamehorn, *Pioneer Steelmaker in the West*. Boulder: Pruett Publishing, 1976.

Barron Beshoar, *Out of the Depths*. Denver: Golden Bell, 1957.

Materials used for chapter 10 include:

Maurice Frink, W. Turrentine Jackson, and Agnes Spring, *When Grass Was King*. Boulder: University of Colorado, 1956.

Ora Peake, *The Colorado Range Cattle Industry*. Glendale: Arthur H. Clarke, 1937.

Alvin Steinel, *History of Agriculture in Colorado*. Fort Collins: State Agricultural College, 1926.

Clark Spence, *The Rainmakers*. Lincoln: University of Nebraska, 1980.

Materials used for chapter 11 include:

Duane Vandenbusche and Duane A. Smith, *A Land Alone*. Boulder: Pruett Publishing, 1981.

Duane A. Smith, *Song of the Hammer and Drill: The Colorado San Juans, 1860–1914*. Golden: Colorado School of Mines, 1982.

Duane A. Smith, *Rocky Mountain Boom Town: A History of Durango*. Albuquerque: University of New Mexico, 1980.

Harriet Backus, *Tomboy Bride*. Boulder: Pruett Publishing, 1969.

Robert Athearn, *Rebel of the Rockies: The Denver and Rio Grande Western*. New Haven: Yale University Press, 1962.

Robert Sloan and Carl Skowronski, *The Rainbow Route*. Denver: Sundance, 1975.

Mallory Hope Ferrell, *Silver San Juan*. Boulder: Pruett Publishing, 1973.

Materials used for chapter 12 include:

Duane A. Smith, *Rocky Mountain Boom Town: A History of Durango*. Albuquerque: University of New Mexico Press, 1980.

Duane A. Smith, *Horace Tabor: His Life and The Legend*. Boulder: Pruett Publishing, 1980. Reprint.

James E. Wright, *The Politics of Populism: Dissent in Colorado*. New Haven: Yale University Press, 1974.

John R. Morris, *Davis H. Waite: The Ideology of a Western Populist*. Washington, D.C., University Press of America, 1982.

Elinor Blumel, "One Hundred Years of Colorado Women," *Colorado Magazine,* Summer 1976.

David L. Lonsdale, "The Fight for an Eight-Hour Day," *Colorado Magazine,* Fall 1966.

The Autobiography of Big Bill Haywood. New York: International Publishers, 1929.

Peter Carlson, *Roughneck: The Life and Times of Big Bill Haywood*. New York: W.W. Norton & Co., 1983.

George C. Suggs, *Colorado's War on Militant Unionism*. Detroit: Wayne State University Press, 1972.

Materials used for chapter 13 include:

Benjamin B. Lindsey, *The Beast*. New York: Doubleday, Page & Co., 1910.

Charles Larsen, *The Good Fight: The Life and Times of Ben B. Lindsey*. Chicago: Quadrangle Books, 1972.

Marjorie Hornbein, "Josephine Roche: Social Worker and Coal Operator," *Colorado Magazine,* Summer 1976.

Elinor Bluemel, *The Opportunity School and Emily Griffith, Its Founder*. Denver: Green Mountain Press, 1970.

Charles A. Johnson, *Denver's Mayor Speer*. Denver: Green Mountain Press, 1969.

Enos A. Mills, *The Spell of the Rockies*. Boston: Houghton-Mifflin, 1911.

E.K. MacColl, "John Franklin Shafroth, Reform Governor of Colorado, 1909–1913," *Colorado Magazine,* January 1952.

Materials used for chapter 14 include:

LeRoy R. Hafen, "The Coming of the Automobile and Improved Roads to Colorado," *Colorado Magazine,* January 1931.

The High Road. Denver: Colorado State Department of Highways, 1976.

Robert A. Goldberg, *Hooded Empire: The Ku Klux Klan in Colorado.* Urbana: University of Illinois Press, 1981.

Marshall Sprague, *Newport in the Rockies: The Life and Good Times of Colorado Springs.* Denver: Sage Books, 1961.

Howard L. Scamehorn, "The First Fifty Years of Flight in Colorado," *University of Colorado Studies,* Series in History, No. 2, November, 1961.

Materials used for chapter 15 include:

Alvin T. Steinel, *History of Agriculture in Colorado.* Fort Collins: Colorado State Agricultural College, 1926.

LeRoy R. Hafen, ed., *Colorado and Its People,* Vol. 1 & 2. New York: Lewis Historical Publishing Co., 1948.

Materials used for chapter 16 include:

Geraldine Bean, *Charles Boettcher: A Study in Pioneer Western Enterprise.* Boulder: Westview Press, 1976.

Thomas J. Noel, *Denver: Rocky Mountain Gold.* Tulsa: Continental Heritage Press, 1980.

William Kostka, Sr., *The Pre-Prohibition History of Adolph Coors Company, 1873–1933.* Golden: Adolph Coors, 1973.

Walter B. and Walter S. Lovelace, *Jesse Shwayder and the Golden Rule.* Denver: Shwayder Bros., 1960.

Woodrow Paige, Jr., *Orange Madness.* New York: Crowell, 1978.

Mark S. Foster, *The Denver Bears: From Sandlots to Sellouts.* Boulder: Pruett Publishing, 1983.

Rodolfo Gonzales, *I Am Joaquin.* New York: Bantam Books, 1972.

Materials used for chapter 17 include:

Richard D. Lamm and Michael McCarthy, *The Angry West.* Boston: Houghton Mifflin, 1982.

Thomas J. Noel, *Denver's Larimer Street: Main Street, Skid Row and Urban Renaissance.* Denver: Historic Denver, Inc., 1981.

Mark S. Foster, "Colorado's Defeat of the 1976 Winter Olympics," *Colorado Magazine,* Spring 1976.

Index